# THE UNFIXED HORIZON

Medbh M

*The Un*

Horizo

Guckian

*fixed*

## NEW SELECTED POEMS

Selected and with an Introduction by
Borbála Faragó and Michaela Schrage-Früh

WAKE FOREST UNIVERSITY PRESS

ISBN 978-1-930630-75-8
Library of Congress Control Number 2015944069

Designed by Quemadura.
Cover image © Jeffrey Morgan.
Used with permission from the Naughton Gallery
Collection of Queen's University Belfast.

The publication of this book was supported
in part by the Boyle Family Fund.

# CONTENTS

*Also in *The Face of the Earth*

†Also in *Had I a Thousand Lives*

‡Also in *Drawing Ballerinas*

# INTRODUCTION[1]

THIS COLLECTION OFFERS a representative selection from Medbh McGuckian's oeuvre, published between 1982 and 2013 and comprising fourteen volumes of poetry to date. Over the course of these thirty-one years, McGuckian has emerged as a major poetic voice and continues to puzzle, challenge, and delight her readers with what Clair Wills has aptly termed her "strange and wonderful work."[2] By retracing the poet's remarkable trajectory, we aim to provide a useful overview as well as to offer some pathways into poems still often considered opaque and enigmatic. Arguably, a great amount of the pleasure derived from reading McGuckian's work owes precisely to her highly original, unconventional writing style, which, in one of her meta-poems, she aptly describes as "a beautiful / season you could never be prepared for . . . a sea-poem in shreds / between your fingers" ("Harvest"). Those readers willing to go with the flow of syntactical structures branching out, of images mutating and multiplying in dream-like fashion, will be gripped by an intimate, sensual, and intense reading experience. Other readers may enjoy reading the poems alongside the sources from which the poet constructs her works, skillfully weaving together strands from typically unacknowledged prose texts.[3] At the same time, these poems, firmly rooted in Northern Irish soil, deeply engage with themes of universal significance, the poet's broad range of topics encompassing subjects as diverse and inextricably entwined as female sexuality, procreation, childbirth, and motherhood; art, creativity, and the creative process; political violence and conflict; home and belonging; aging, death, mourning, and spirituality.

Medbh McGuckian's poetic career was launched in 1979 when her poem "The Flitting" won the British National Poetry Competition. The controversy surrounding the events following McGuckian's nomination is indicative of the political and gender issues complicating her early career and reception. McGuckian had submitted her work under the English-sounding, gender-ambiguous pseudonym Jean Fisher. When eventually it became obvious that the prize of this prestigious national competition had been awarded to an unknown, highly pregnant schoolteacher from Belfast, the committee decided to split the prize money of £1000 and give half of it to the more renowned English male poet who had come second. Nevertheless, the prize and ensuing media attention opened up hitherto closed doors: after her first poems appeared in two chapbooks—*Single Ladies: Sixteen Poems* (Interim Press, 1980) and *Portrait of Joanna* (Ulsterman, 1980)—McGuckian signed a book contract with Oxford University Press, where her first major collection, *The Flower Master* (1982),[4] was published.

The critical response to this debut collection was striking in that her readership was immediately split into those who dismissed her work as "alluring sort of nonsense"[5] and those who openly confessed to "admiring what [they] cannot understand."[6] Crucially, her exploration of nature and domestic images as well as traditional female craft, which in turn "disguised" recurrent themes of pregnancy, childbirth, and motherhood, led many critics to categorize McGuckian's early work as essentially private, domestic, and exclusively concerned with "female" issues. Based on this perception, the majority of critics mistakenly tended to label McGuckian's work as non-political, thereby excluding her from discourses on Northern Irish identity. At the same time, her supposed lack of engagement with the Troubles was deemed evasive, if not escapist, in a poet who was born and had spent all her life in Belfast. What many critics failed to grasp, however, was that McGuckian's multi-layered poems characteristically interweave the private and the public, viewing the sectarian violence in her native Belfast through the lens of the female body as well as through elaborate domestic and nature images—while they *do* tell all the truth, these poems most certainly tell it *slant*. In an interview, McGuckian sums up the "complex agenda" that determined her early writing years:

My Northern Catholicism isolated me triply, not just in terms of my gender. The three crises interwove but oscillated in importance, and certainly being a Catholic was much more a matter of life and death at that time than being a woman or being a Northerner, so it probably took precedence. At the same time, what I was going through personally as a woman—pregnancy, childbirth, acute post-natal depression—were the main experiences described, and these are painted against the terrible backdrop of daily and nightly murder.[7]

Arguably, then, McGuckian's early poetry not only opens up a rich, unpredictable, and sensually conveyed world of feminine sensibility, but provides a female poet's perspective on issues such as Northern Irish identity and the Troubles. A good example is her short poem "Eavesdropper,"[8] in which the central image of "a bullet / left in me" encodes a girl's onset of menstruation, suggesting how a hostile environment affects and pervades the girl's sense of self to such an extent that she internalizes Northern Ireland's sectarian division and its ensuing violence. By means of intricate imagery and color symbolism, the dense, multi-layered poem exemplifies how struggling to come to terms with one's bewildering sexual, national, and religious identity triggers the creative impulse from which the poem emerges. Since "Eavesdropper" focuses on the female poet's coming of age in the specific Northern Irish context, it may be read as McGuckian's poetic response to Seamus Heaney's "Digging," which explores similar themes from a male poet's perspective.

McGuckian's second collection, *Venus and the Rain* (1984), continues and expands these themes by revising static and stereotypical representations of women in poetry and art. Thus, in "Hotel," one of her numerous meta-poems, the stereotypical "damsel in distress" is rejected for "a name / with a hundred meanings, all of them / secret, going their own way." Other poems allude to canonical works by male writers, notably "The Rising Out," which responds to Yeats's "Easter 1916" and Rilke's "Requiem für eine Freundin" ["Requiem for a Friend"] from the dual perspective of artist and mother: "My dream sister has gone into my blood / to kill the poet in me before Easter." The poet's inability to write during her pregnancy, her experience of severe postpartum depression after her first son's birth in 1980, and the struggle to balance the roles of mother, daughter, wife, and poet are at the heart of this and other poems. Although the poetic speaker in "The Rising Out" physically and mentally experiences the fragmentation of her body and self, and, on a metaphorical level, internalizes the division of her country, her tension is resolved in the end. She neither dies, as does the woman-artist in Rilke's poem, nor does she turn into a Mother-Ireland figure sacrificing her children so that "a terrible beauty" can be born, as suggested by Yeats's poem. Instead, she bears a child whose existence temporarily prevents, but ultimately inspires and molds her poetic work. Motherhood, then, becomes not only a metaphor for poetic creation, but the very source from which it derives:

> If she had died suddenly I would have heard
> blood stretched on the frame, though her dream
> is the same seed that lifted me out of my clothes
> and carried me till it saw itself as fruit. ("The Rising Out")

Unsurprisingly, McGuckian's unique style, characterized by playfulness, ambiguity, and flux, has been read in terms of various theories of *écriture féminine* and is indeed well suited to the subversion and revision of conventional, simplified representations of women and femininity. At the same time, this Northern Irish poet's declared aim is to create an "un-English language" ("The Partners' Desk"). This becomes particularly obvious in McGuckian's third collection, *On Ballycastle Beach* (1988), in which English, the colonizer's tongue, is "Europeanized" as well as "Hibernicized." This is why McGuckian, to use the poet's own phrase from this volume, is often seen as "a threader / of double-stranded words" ("The Dream-Language of Fergus"). Several poems included in the collection are patchworks composed of phrases borrowed from English translations of Eastern European writers' essays, letters, journals, and biographies. The poet's discovery and exploration of historical similarities between Northern Ireland and the political contexts in which writers such as Osip Mandelstam and Marina Tsvetaeva lived and worked is depicted as a reinvigorating experience that culminates in a "European feeling which now blows about, / a cream-coloured blossom, with a blue vigour" ("Balakhana"). At the same time, the collection is also more openly concerned with contested space and place and, again, with intersections of the private and the political. The title refers to a small town on the North Antrim coast, simultaneously the birthplace of McGuckian's father and the childhood home of Irish nationalist Roger Casement (1864–1916). It is also McGuckian's place of refuge from the tensions in Belfast. Symbolically, then, Ballycastle provides a stark contrast to the sectarian, walled-in Belfast, a place inimical to the international perspective the collection seeks to achieve. *On Ballycastle Beach* explores the context of home in both personal and political terms and is permeated by a sense of rootedness. At the same time, recurrent images of ships and airplanes suggest the poet's mental journeys and dreamlike flights of the imagination as well as her opening out to European influences. Commenting on the numerous travels she embarked on after becoming a full-time writer in 1985, the poet explains:

> Reading European history and actually visiting Germany, Spain, France, Holland, Portugal, also Japan, Sweden, made me aware how ignorant and benighted my education has been. I still have not been deep into Russia but have learned from its four major poets the limits of our suffering under imperial rule. I especially love Lorca and Mandelstam for their direct sacrifices. Most of *On Ballycastle Beach* has to do with this opening out to influences beyond England as if the island had shadowed me, although I still acknowledge the gifts.

The title of McGuckian's fourth collection, *Marconi's Cottage* (1991), refers to a cottage situated on Ballycastle Beach, which was owned by McGuckian at the time of writing the *Marconi* poems. It is also the cottage in which the Irish-Italian scientist Guglielmo Marconi (1874–1937) experimented with the transmission of wireless messages over water. The cottage, then, serves as an adequate symbol for McGuckian's intertextual dialogues across space and time with what could be seen as an "imagined community" of international women writers and artists, including Paula Modersohn-Becker ("To Call Paula Paul"), Tatyana Tolstoy ("A Small Piece of Wood"), Emily Brontë ("Gigot Sleeves"),

Emily Dickinson ("The Most Emily of All"), Anne Devlin ("The Unplayed Rosalind"), and numerous others. By incorporating quotations from these writers' and artists' biographies, journals, or correspondence into her poems, McGuckian not only explores and assuages her need for female literary precursors but highlights the difficulties and isolation shared by women writing and creating art in hostile socio-cultural environments. At the heart of the collection is a double concern with birth and death, which autobiographically reflects the poet's experience of giving birth to her daughter Emer while emotionally preparing for her father's impending death. The metaphysical implications of the idea of rebirth are explored against the backdrop of the ongoing sectarian violence in Northern Ireland. Images of destruction and war permeate the collection, culminating in the most horrible and surreal image of a smashed embryo:

> . . . That dream
> of a too early body undamaged
> and beautiful, head smashed to pulp,
> still grows in my breakfast cup. . . ("No Streets, No Numbers")

However, the desperate and nightmarish atmosphere evoked by such images is counterbalanced by poems celebrating the birth of the poet's long-wished-for daughter, an event seen as fulfilling and potentially redemptive. As she puts it in "Oval of a Girl": "But one discarnate shadow / can be worth a whole generation; I am flooded / by no ocean but a second you."

The course of opening out characterizes McGuckian's three collections succeeding *Marconi's Cottage*, in that the poet embraces and explores her country's past and present more overtly. *Captain Lavender* (1994) deals with the double theme of her father's death and with her experience of teaching political prisoners at the Maze Prison. Both the dead father and the prisoners are repeatedly feminized throughout the collection, which the poet explains as follows:

> [I]t seems to me that the North itself has all the complexes of a powerless woman, and the male Catholic writer within it is impotent, castrated, victimised, reduced. I see this affecting my father and sons, my husband and brothers, and most dramatically the hunger-strikers and long-term prisoners who were writing poetry as a "terrorist" outlet. However, in *Captain Lavender* I was less overtly working out my relationships with politics than dealing with the loss of the parent of the opposite gender, the death of that maleness within me or its source, and so it was a psychosexual journey which brought these other insights in its wake. The ones I had been led to fear as brutal and masculine I came upon disarmed and vulnerable.

"The Aisling Hat" describes the deceased father as "intoxicated like a woman," while "Flirting with Saviours" depicts the political prisoners as "men utterly outside themselves, with the taint of women." At times, McGuckian's speakers adopt the role of *Éire* or a *spéirbhean* figure, as in "The Over Mother" or "Flirting with Saviours." In other poems, such as "Elegy for an Irish

Speaker," she rivals "Miss Death," clearly a negative version of Cathleen Ní Houlihan, who is "waiting to be fertilized" by the death of the speaker's father. The most poignant piece in the collection is arguably the uncharacteristically short title poem, "Captain Lavender," in which the poet is charting the unknown territory of a daughter's grief for her father:

> Night-hours. The edge of a fuller moon
> waits among the interlocking patterns
> of a flier's sky.
>
> Sperm names, ovum names, push inside
> each other. We are half-taught
> our real names, from other lives.
>
> Emphasise your eyes. Be my flare-
> path, my uncold begetter,
> my air-minded bird-sense.

The complex story behind this poem, beautifully elucidated by McGuckian, is worth quoting at length:

> The speaker is myself in the persona of Beryl Markham who was in love with Denys Finch Hatton in *Out of Africa*, and when he died in a flying accident got over him by learning to fly and was the first woman to fly alone from London to Nova Scotia. So I imagine that solo flight as a love-death-exorcism. She has no light and no runway to land so the beloved's eyes have to lead her. *Captain Lavender* is

the reverse of the *Flower Master* title. It's like in the first book I was a woman asserting male equality in writing poetry; here I am a man being restored to the femininity of nature. In many songs of rebellion in Ireland, death is addressed as a military sergeant or captain. [ ... ] It's quite a disturbing reflection in that the dead father is asked to woo the masculinised daughter as a seductive woman might and thus re-conceive her in a new form or be re-conceived by her. There is also an Icarus element in there as Beryl crash-landed and was quite injured. But it is mapping a voyage into uncharted territory and possibilities of connections beyond the flesh and time. [ ... ] It's like the grieving process and very solitary and a dangerous pioneer form of travel, unaided.

McGuckian's sixth collection, *Shelmalier* (1998), focuses on Irish history even more overtly. The collection explores the 1798 Rebellion and relates the poet's own learning process about her country's rebellious history, which enabled her "to welcome into consciousness figures of an integrity [she] had never learned to be proud of" (Author's Note to *Shelmalier*). Her approach to the historical events is thus a deeply personal one, as she explores the emotional impact and legacy of the past, as in "The Feastday of Peace," where "the long, long dead / steer with their warmed breath / my unislanded dreams." The historical events and figures, then, are filtered through the poet's creative subconscious, her dreams, while political commentary and rhetoric is deliberately avoided. Instead, the figures of the United Irishmen fighting and dying for Ireland's freedom are "resurrected" in, at times, romanticized or eroticized encounters, often playing upon traditional gendered representations of Ireland, as in "Stone with Potent Figure," which envisions Ireland as a girl "buried / weaponless in her coffin"—sleeping rather than dead.

Similarly, *Drawing Ballerinas* (2001), McGuckian's seventh collection, centers on the Troubles as well as the onset of the Northern Irish Peace Process in the wake of the 1998 Good Friday Agreement. As McGuckian informs us in a footnote, the title poem refers to a quotation by the French painter Matisse who, "when asked how he managed to survive World War II artistically, replied that he spent the worst years 'drawing ballerinas.'" McGuckian thus implicitly answers back to those critics reproaching her for supposedly ignoring the civil war around her. Although the poem describes one of Matisse's ballerina drawings, her description presents the dancing girl as the victim of a bomb explosion:

> The body turns in, restless, on itself, in
> a womb of sleep, an image of isolated sleep.
> It turns over, reveals opposing versions of itself,
> one arm broken abruptly at elbow and wrist,
> the other wrenched downwards by the force of the turning.
>     ("Drawing Ballerinas")

The poem, as its footnote further informs us, commemorates "Ann Frances Owens, schoolfellow and neighbour, who lost her life in the Abercorn Café explosion, 1972." As this poem poignantly illustrates, the legacy of the Troubles, though at times concealed and disguised, is deeply entwined with Medbh McGuckian's beautiful and enigmatic poems. Or, as the epigraph to *Captain Lavender*, a quotation from Picasso, says: "I have not painted the war . . . but I have no doubt that the war is in . . . these paintings I have done."

If "the war" is implicit in McGuckian's poems up to *Drawing Ballerinas*, it arguably moves center stage in her next collection, a volume published in North America by Wake Forest University Press and aptly titled *The Soldiers of Year II* (2002). Twenty-two of the seventy-six poems also appeared in *Drawing Ballerinas*, while some of the rest were published in *The Face of the Earth* (2002) and *Had I a Thousand Lives* (2003), brought out by The Gallery Press. *The Soldiers of Year II*, however, is a volume with a strong and coherent thematic focus, concentrating on the effects of violence on the body and soul. Although the poet alludes to historical atrocities such as the Great Famine, the World Wars, or the Troubles, her attention is on the present, in particular on the ways in which language can process trauma. As Guinn Batten aptly describes in her "Afterword" to the collection:

No longer choosing between either the secret, unexamined, sometimes unconscious interiors of a sexualized and often female self or the public, historical heroes that are invited into that self as she did in *Shelmalier*, McGuckian now dwells more disturbingly in these poems at the very intersections of power with the bodies that record its mandates. Skeptical in particular of the command of peace, these poems look closely at those who are victims or beneficiaries of change during an uncertain, transitional period. More often than not, in the *The Soldiers of Year II* the body becomes collective, a heterogeneous community glued together by a shared suffering but also by a shared hope.[9]

The opening prose poem, "Helen's War," introduces this concept. The piece mentions a debilitating three-year illness, and also hints at war, merging public and private traumas that are equally difficult to process. The word "die" occurs six times in different contexts, but the text does not limit time or characters, hinting at the pervasiveness of suffering. The poem ends with the speaker attempting to take the anonymous addressee back in time:

> Once I wanted to take you down the lane to the haunted house, the fairies' house, we would have had a great day, but she wouldn't let me take you through the grass in case you got your feet wet. We were just setting off, when she gave this cry, or shriek, from the gate, and so we had to turn back.

The presence of pain and the "shriek" of the mother halt the process of remembering, and the "haunted house" of memory remains unvisited while the ordeal is still acutely experienced. Going back in time is only possible if the violence of illness, death, and political upheaval is accepted, owned, and articulated; otherwise re-living these experiences renews the suffering.

Dealing with the anguish of the past is also the subject of "Love Affair with Firearms," which in its title calls attention to the paradox of remembering: it heals but also risks re-inscribing the pain, like an epitaph or an obituary.

> From behind the moon boys' graves
> bleed endlessly; from photograph
> to browning photograph they blacken
> headlines, stranded outside of time
> at the story's frigid edge.

The act of recollection brings the speaker "right back where we were / before the world turned over" into the moment precipitating violence, a process which "shovels up / fresh pain" alongside the "long-stemmed roses" of healing. The central challenge of the poem is the demand of recovery through the passing of time in order to write lovingly about victims of violence without allowing anger and hurt to overwhelm the process. *The Soldiers of Year II* suggests, however, that this is difficult if not impossible, and that memory is often no more than a resurrection of the emotional trauma that follows in the wake of the incident. The volume is a melodic meditation on memory, the "winged death with two conversing / skeletons" ("A Religion of Writing") that accompanies commemoration and personal recollection of harrowing events.

McGuckian's following three volumes, *The Face of the Earth* (2002), *Had I a Thousand Lives* (2003), and *The Book of the Angel* (2004), concluded an especially prolific period. While the violence of the previous decade was largely absent, during these years the fragility of the peace-process was all too apparent, and genuine confidence about the durability of the peace was frequently difficult to sustain. The political violence experienced through the Troubles arose in thematic, allegorical forms in McGuckian's more overtly political volumes, *Captain Lavender* and *Shelmalier*. *Drawing Ballerinas* signalled the arrival of a new thematic voice and interest in McGuckian's work, reflecting on the Troubles from a more internalized, almost philosophical perspective. The succeeding three collections continue with this theme, allowing the experienced violence and darkness to surface in an increasingly spiritual tone. Religion and faith appear as comfort and creative impetus, suffusing McGuckian's language with otherworldly and sacred imagery. Religion as a thematic focus follows the meditative reflections of *The Soldiers of Year II* and leads the poet back to contemplating the creative self. In *The Face of the Earth, Had I a Thousand Lives*, and *The Book of The Angel*, death, spirituality, and religion become the source of creative performance, where divinity enters and reconfigures McGuckian's poetic language.

*The Face of the Earth* focuses on spiritual renewal through corporeal and natural images. The epigraph, taken from the *Psalms*, is: "Thou sendest forth thy spirit, they are created: and thou renewest the face of the earth." The face of the earth becomes the surface that bears the scars of the past, yet it still needs renewal. The question, then, in both political and poetic terms, is whether rejuvenation is indeed possible or whether it remains an illusion. Here, the focus shifts to nature and its innate ability to revivify death and decay. In political terms, the collection considers ideas of progress and their relevance to the individual. And yet, *The Face of the Earth* also marks a return to the themes of McGuckian's earlier volumes. Images of nature and the female body as sites of identity evoke poems like "Isba Song" or "Lime Trees in Winter, Retouched" from *Venus and the Rain*, but the creative performance is centered on absence: "I kept colliding with the absence" ("High Altitude Lavender"). A deep-seated unease permeates the volume. Words arrange themselves arbitrarily and the contribution of the author appears almost involuntary: "My hand made a shining journey of its own" ("Christmas Eve Sky"). In terms of McGuckian's politicized aesthetics, this volume signals a temporary departure from a more overt political vocabulary.

*Had I a Thousand Lives* returns to some of McGuckian's earlier interests as well. Written for the bicentenary of the execution of Robert Emmet and Thomas Russell in 1803, the volume imaginatively appropriates the "saintly" figures of Irish nationalist iconography to contemplate death and political sacrifice. The focus is not purely ideological though, as the collection avoids direct commentary and political analysis. Rather, these poems suggest questions of identity and belonging through romanticized communion with Ireland's dead. It is in their death that Emmet and Russell "come alive," and in this volume death, in fact, becomes the driving force of the creative performance. The imagery of death in *Had I a Thousand Lives* characterizes the dynamics of identity formation. Identity, interpreted here as a construct of continual change and development, incorporates its own undoing. The political pressures of identity formation evoke a poetical response through reshuffling conventional metaphors of self. Death is no longer interpreted only as the ultimate obliteration of life. Seen as a threshold, death gains center stage as the ultimate space and time that define human and poetic expression. McGuckian comments: "Death is not something that should be used as an excuse for not saying things. Life is short."[10]

*The Book of the Angel* offers a departure within McGuckian's oeuvre. In this collection dedicated to angels, McGuckian reconsiders issues of religion, spirituality, and identity. The volume resolves some of the complicated issues at the heart of McGuckian's relationship to her Catholic faith:

Personal Catholicism is an ideal I try to follow, but the social persecution of the false minority created here has perhaps made me polemical and narrowed my focus or made me bitter. I have found it a relief to go back to pre-reformation Dante for example. The Church's attitude to women was in my experience a very damaging coldness that took me a long time to recover from, if I have. On the other hand, the beauty and aspiration and comfort of the rituals and prayer have been a vital support. Specifically in *The Book of the Angel* I have been fascinated by the doctrines of the Eucharist and the Incarnation, and although the trial of Christ has always corresponded with my sense of Ireland's injustice and tragedy, the Resurrection, as with Yeats, has always given suffering a meaning and made living here, in the sense of the North and this world, possible.

In the Old Irish text, *Liber Angeli*, or "Book of the Angel," Saint Patrick discusses his ecclesiastical position in Armagh with an angel. Appropriating this title for her collection, McGuckian meditates on three elements of this eighth-century inheritance: religion, national identity, and, most importantly, its unique, metaphysical composition as dialogue between the divine and the secular. The central figure of the angel becomes the embodiment of transition. The angel's gender, as well as its language, occupies the in-between spaces of the poetic imagination, connecting a powerful divine presence to a stubbornly real sense of self. The angels who occupy these poems and accompany the reader on a spiritualized journey remain ungraspable and shapeless, though lovingly humanized transient creatures: "Words remain on the shore, but when the angel / falls in love, with his different prayer movements, // he is the perfect human" ("Poem Rhyming in 'J'"). Prayer becomes an alternative language of poetic and political expression, placing the act of composition in the context of divine creation. For McGuckian, the unstable speaking (praying) self becomes the recipient of communication, simultaneously distanced as divine and approached as human. The reader becomes positioned within the process of prayer; thus reading, too, becomes praying, the angel becomes the messenger. This kind of poetic prayer is secular and humanist, however, and the central idea of disrupting patterns of communication remains dominant. Ultimately, *The Book of the Angel* signals a deepening of themes in the earlier volumes in its daring, yet subversive, engagement with overt Catholic iconography.

In her last three volumes published to date, McGuckian revisits some of her earlier themes and simultaneously conducts a retrospective journey through her creative oeuvre. *The Currach Requires No Harbours* (2006) and *My Love Has Fared Inland* (2008) are both collections about journeying, while *The High Caul Cap* (2012) explores loss and disintegration.

In a manner similar to the two preceding volumes, *The Currach Requires No Harbours* considers the effects and meanings of political violence. The collection was born out of the violence McGuckian's daughter Emer experienced in Belfast one day coming home from school, which had a profound effect on the poet. McGuckian recounted the details of the event in an interview:

> This bus [the school-bus] would take all the children to begin with, but would then drop off the Protestant children in the Protestant area, and then ferry the Catholics up to the more Catholic districts. It's very clear where that border is. The bus was attacked there. All

the Protestants got of and attacked the bus because they knew there were only Catholics left. Emer got a brick thrown at her head. She took an epileptic fit. It had hit her eye.[11]

The traumatic effect of this sectarian violence makes *The Currach Requires No Harbours* a heavily politicized volume. The first sixteen poems of the collection reflect on her daughter's injury and on the poet's personal struggle to come to terms with the seemingly unchanged violent landscape in which she lives. Seeing and blindness are central concepts here that shape the poet's understanding of politics, religion, and family responsibilities. However, *The Currach Requires No Harbours* is arguably also a book about women, and the second part of the volume shifts the focus to older women and explores the metaphor of the house in this context. In these poems, the poetic psyche is both the observing and the suffering subject and the reader is invited to share this doubled perspective. The verses reflect on the effects of political violence, but there is no morality and no didactic teaching. The poems, like hurt bodies, are simply there, presenting mortality and pain.

*My Love Has Fared Inland* promises a definite inward journey in its title. Taking up familiar themes of creativity and spirituality, the poems trace an introspective voyage the reader is not always invited to join. McGuckian returns to the language and linguistic difficulty of her earliest volumes with metaphors that are self-reflexive, introverted, and resistant to easy paraphrase. The epigraph warns that sound has to abandon "the servile function of signification" to become "vital and its own excuse for being." We are not invited to interpret, but only to enjoy the words "freely as music." As often is the case with McGuckian, however, there is a thematic coherence that points beyond the linguistic difficulty. The volume's poems float, dispersed among a variety of themes. Death, writing, nature, and love all play a part, brought together by the recurring motif of inward movement. This private journey is driven by suffering and authorial anxiety, and its meditations on death echo the poet's earlier work on this subject. Non-consequential action, futility, and dead ends epitomize a voice which exists only for itself. This minimalistic, dark tone is at the crux of McGuckian's poetic expression in this volume, which foregrounds ideas of passivity, failure, and futility. "South of Mars" opens with a linguistic closure: "It's over now. Part of the story / has disappeared, into the void / of something that has ended forever." The poem describes loss and a "sadness that slackens electrical lines." Most tellingly it muses that "perhaps / what we thought would cast a thick shadow // will cast none at all." Whether this is about leaving a poetic mark or personal anxiety, "casting a shadow" becomes a recurring motif throughout the volume.

McGuckian's latest volume, *The High Caul Cap* (2012), deals with death, loss, and the struggle to come to terms with grief. The poems chart the poet's progress from the helplessness of watching her mother's body deteriorate to mourning her death and trying to come to terms with life without her, ending with imagining the already-departed soul's impressions on life. "Dormition: Madonna with Trees" attempts to accompany the mother on her "disintegrating voyage." At the poem's end, the dying mother stands alone, anchored in her life, while her loved ones hold on and "go beyond her," into the abyss of death:

> Now all of the bodies
>
> stand to one edge of the drapery,
> without releasing, go beyond her,
> so that she may stall and anchor there.

The mother dies as quietly as she lived, softly slipping away from her family. What has changed is her child's encounter with oblivion, which alters her relationship with the mother. The dying process is also a process of love that embraces that void, rather than turning away from it. Like the famous *Pietà*, the poem gives us an example of how love can make sense of death, an idea that stands at the center of this collection. The book provides both a haunting and a haunted gaze: it sees and shows everything, courageously accompanying the body on its journey of decline. The poems are populated by images of loss, blindness, illness, and other types of atrophy, which the human gaze usually avoids. They also explore ideas of spirituality, interiority, and love in order to counter those images of the abyss.

In her volumes published to date, Medbh McGuckian takes us on an extraordinary journey. Encompassing private, domestic, and feminine, as well as political, spiritual, and philosophical concerns, her multi-layered work engages with issues that resonate with readers across continents. At the same time, McGuckian's unique poetic style renders her one of the most compelling voices in contemporary poetry in English. Her unusual method of composition, weaving together strands from various prose texts, turns her poems into strangely original, dreamlike creations, both haunted and haunting. The present selection offers a glimpse into the depth and diversity of the poet's exceptionally creative oeuvre. It is our hope that these poems will reach readers who are interested in the multifaceted landscape of contemporary Northern Irish poetry, and also those who look to be challenged and engaged on a creative, linguistic, and philosophical level.

BORBÁLA FARAGÓ AND
MICHAELA SCHRAGE-FRÜH

## *Notes*

1. Parts of this introduction are based on the editors' previously published work on Medbh McGuckian, most notably: Michaela Schrage-Früh, *Emerging Identities: Myth, Nation and Gender in the Poetry of Eavan Boland, Nuala Ní Dhomhnaill and Medbh McGuckian* (Trier: Wissenschaftlicher Verlag Trier, 2004) and Borbála Faragó, *Medbh McGuckian* (Maryland: Bucknell University Press and Cork: Cork University Press, 2014).

2. Clair Wills, "Afterword," *The Poetry of Medbh McGuckian: The Interior of Words*, ed. Richard Kirkland and Shane Alcobia-Murphy (Cork: Cork University Press, 2010), 213.

3. Medbh McGuckian typically constructs her poems out of quotations from unacknowledged sources, such as prose texts, biographies, journals, letters, or critical works. Reading her poetry alongside these sources, many of which have by now been identified, can facilitate new insights and levels of meaning. For a full appreciation of McGuckian's intertextual method and its functions, see Shane Alcobia-Murphy, *Medbh McGuckian: The Poetics of Exemplarity* (University of Aberdeen: AHRC Centre for Irish and Scottish Studies, 2012).

4. All dates given are first publication dates. See bibliography for publication details for this and other volumes by McGuckian.

5. James Simmons, "A Literary Leg-Pull?" *Belfast Review* 8 (1984): 27.

6. Cf. Peggy O'Brien, "Reading Medbh McGuckian: Admiring What We Cannot Understand," *Colby Quarterly* 28.4 (1992): 239–50.

7. Unless otherwise indicated, this and all following quotations from Medbh McGuckian are taken from an unpublished interview conducted by Michaela Schrage-Früh in 2004.

8. This poem was originally published under the title "That Year" but was renamed "Eavesdropper" in *The Flower Master and Other Poems* (The Gallery Press, 1993). Some of the poems included in the re-edited collection (such as "Smoke") carry more overtly political overtones, a change that may also be attributed to McGuckian's decision to cease her collaboration with Oxford University Press and sign a contract with Irish publisher The Gallery Press.

9. Guinn Batten, "Afterword," *The Soldiers of Year II* (Winston-Salem: Wake Forest University Press, 2002), 126.

10. María Jesús Lorenzo Modia, "An Interview with Medbh McGuckian," *The European English Messenger* 13.2 (Autumn 2004): 40.

11. Shane Alcobia-Murphy and Richard Kirkland, "Interview with Medbh McGuckian," *The Poetry of Medbh McGuckian*, ed. Shane Alcobia-Murphy and Richard Kirkland (Cork: Cork University Press, 2010), 205.

# The Flower Master and Other Poems

# SMOKE

They set the whins on fire along the road.
I wonder what controls it, can the wind hold
that snake of orange motion to the hills,
away from the houses?

They seem so sure what they can do.
I am unable even
to contain myself, I run
till the fawn smoke settles on the earth.

# THE 'SINGER'

In the evenings I used to study
at my mother's old sewing-machine,
pressing my feet occasionally
up and down on the treadle
as though I were going somewhere
I had never been.

Every year at exams, the pressure mounted—
the summer light bent across my pages
like a squinting eye. The children's shouts
echoed the weather of the street,
a car was thunder,
the ticking of a clock was heavy rain. . . .

In the dark I drew the curtains
on young couples stopping in the entry,
heading home. There were nights
I sent the disconnected wheel
spinning madly round and round
till the empty bobbin rattled in its case.

# EAVESDROPPER

That year it was something to do with your hands:
to play about with rings, to harness rhythm
in staging bleach or henna on the hair,
or shackling, unshackling the breasts.

I remembered as a child the red kite
lost forever over our heads, the white ball
a pin-prick on the tide, and studied
the leaf-patterned linoleum, the elaborate

stitches on my pleated bodice.
It was like a bee's sting or a bullet
left in me, this mark, this sticking pins in dolls,
listening for the red and white

particles of time to trickle slow, like a wet nurse
feeding nonchalantly someone else's child.
I wanted curtainings, and cushionings;
the grass is an eavesdropper's bed.

# MR MCGREGOR'S GARDEN

Some women save their sanity with needles.
I complicate my life with studies
of my favourite rabbit's head, his vulgar volatility,
or a little ladylike sketching
of my resident toad in his flannel box;
or search for handsome fungi for my tropical
herbarium, growing dry-rot in the garden,
and wishing that the climate were kinder,
turning over the spiky purple heads among the moss
with my cheese-knife to view the slimy veil.

Unlike the cupboard-love of sleepers in the siding,
my hedgehog's sleep is under his control
and not the weather's; he can rouse himself
at half-an-hour's notice in the frost, or leave at will
on a wet day in August, by the hearth.
He goes by breathing slowly, after a large meal,
a lively evening, very cross if interrupted,
and returns with a hundred respirations
to the minute, weak and nervous when he wakens,
busy with his laundry.

On sleepless nights while learning
Shakespeare off by heart,
I feel that Bunny's at my bedside
in a white cotton nightcap,
tickling me with his whiskers.

# SLIPS

The studied poverty of a moon roof,
the earthenware of dairies cooled by apple trees,
the apple tree that makes the whitest wash . . .

But I forget names, remembering them wrongly
where they touch upon another name,
a town in France like a woman's Christian name.

My childhood is preserved as a nation's history,
my favourite fairytales the shells
leased by the hermit crab.

I see my grandmother's death as a piece of ice,
my mother's slimness restored to her,
my own key slotted in your door—

tricks you might guess from this unfastened button,
a pen mislaid, a word misread,
my hair coming down in the middle of a conversation.

# THE HOLLYWOOD BED

We narrow into the house, the room, the bed,
where sleep begins its shunting. You adopt
your mask, your intellectual cradling of the head,
neat as notepaper in your creaseless
envelope of clothes, while I lie crosswise,
imperial as a favoured only child,
calmed by sagas of how we lay like spoons
in a drawer, till you blew open
my tightened bud, my fully-buttoned housecoat,
like some Columbus mastering
the saw-toothed waves, the rows of letter *m*s.

Now the headboard is disturbed
by your uncomfortable skew, your hands
like stubborn adverbs visiting your face,
or your shoulder, in your piquancy of dreams,
the outline that, if you were gone,
would find me in your place.

# THE SOFA

Do not be angry if I tell you
your letter stayed unopened on my table
for several days. If you were friend enough
to believe me, I was about to start writing
at any moment; my mind was savagely made up,
like a serious sofa moved
under a north window. My heart, alas,

is not the calmest of places.
Still it is not my heart that needs replacing:
and my books seem real enough to me,
my disasters, my surrenders, all my loss. . . .
Since I was child enough to forget
that you loathe poetry, you ask for some—
about nature, greenery, insects, and, of course,

the sun—surely that would be to open
an already open window? To celebrate
the impudence of flowers? If I could
interest you instead in his large, gentle stares,
how his soft shirt is the inside of pleasure
to me, why I must wear white for him,
imagine he no longer trembles

when I approach, no longer buys me
flowers for my name day. . . . But I spread
on like a house, I begin to scatter
to a tiny to-and-fro at odds
with the wear on my threshold. Somewhere
a curtain rising wonders where I am,
my books sleep, pretending to forget me.

# THE SEED-PICTURE

This is my portrait of Joanna—since the split
the children come to me like a dumb-waiter,
and I wonder where to put them, beautiful seeds
with no immediate application . . . the clairvoyance
of seed-work has opened up
new spectrums of activity, beyond a second home.
The seeds dictate their own vocabulary,
their dusty colours capture
more than we can plan,
the mould on walls, or jumbled garages,
dead flower heads where insects shack. . . .
I only guide them not by guesswork
in their necessary numbers,
and attach them by the spine to a perfect bedding,
woody orange pips, and tear-drop apple,
the banana of the caraway, wrinkled peppercorns,
the pocked peach, or waterlily honesty,
the seamed cherry stone so hard to break.

Was it such self-indulgence to enclose her
in the border of a grandmother's sampler,
bonding all the seeds in one continuous skin,
the sky resolved to a cloud the length of a man?

To use tan linseed for the trees, spiky
sunflower for leaves, bright lentils
for the window, patna stars
for the floral blouse? Her hair
is made of hook-shaped marigold, gold
of pleasure for her lips, like raspberry grain.
The eyelids oatmeal, the irises
of Dutch blue maw, black rape
for the pupils, millet
for the vicious beige circles underneath.
The single pearl barley
that sleeps around her dullness
till it catches light, makes women
feel their age, and sigh for liberation.

# THE SOIL-MAP

I am not a woman's man, but I can tell,
by the swinging of your two-leaf door,
you are never without one man in the shadow
of another; and because the mind
of a woman between two men is lighter
than a spark, the petalled steps to your porch
feel frigid with a lost warmth. I will not
take you in hardness, for all the dark cage
of my dreaming over your splendid fenestration,
your moulded sills, your slender purlins,

the secret woe of your gutters. I will do it
without niggardliness, like food with one
generous; a moment as auspicious
and dangerous as the christening of a ship,
my going in to find the settlement
of every floor, the hump of water
following the moon, and her discolouring,
the saddling derangement of a roof
that might collapse its steepness
under the sudden strain of clearing its name.

For anyone with patience can divine
how your plasterwork has lost key, the rendering
about to come away. So like a rainbird,
challenged by a charm of goldfinch,
I appeal to the god who fashions edges
whether such turning-points exist
as these saltings we believe we move
away from, as if by simply shaking
a cloak we could disbud ourselves,
dry out, and cease to live there?

I have found the places on the soil-map,
proving it possible once more to call
houses by their names, Annsgift or Mavisbank,
Mount Juliet or Bettysgrove: they should not
lie with the gloom of disputes to interrupt them
every other year, like some disease
of language making humorous the friendship
of the thighs. I drink to you as Hymenstown,
(my touch of fantasy) or First Fruits,
impatient for my power as a bride.

# THE SUNBENCH

Behind my party wall what bolts of silk
prepare their images, relax from them
like petals lolling in a knot garden
voluptuous with rapid growth! These seed leaves
I have summered and these true leaves wintered
through the spartan frost, supported by sweet
chestnut, riven oak, till lime unlocks
their mongrel tenderness, the shattering excretion of the rose. . . .

This is not the hardness of a single night,
a rib that I could clearly do without. It is
the room where you have eaten daily,
shaking free like a hosting tree, the garden
shaking off the night's weak appetite,
the sunbench brown and draining into fallow.

# THE FLOWER MASTER

Like foxgloves in the school of the grass moon
we come to terms with shade, with the principle
of enfolding space. Our scissors in brocade,
we learn the coolness of straight edges, how
to stroke gently the necks of daffodils
and make them throw their heads back to the sun.

We slip the thready stems of violets, delay
the loveliness of the hibiscus dawn with quiet ovals,
spirals of feverfew like water splashing,
the papery legacies of bluebells. We do
sea-fans with sea-lavender, moon-arrangements
roughly for the festival of moon-viewing.

This black container calls for sloes, sweet
sultan, dainty nipplewort, in honour
of a special guest who, summoned to the
tea ceremony, must stoop to our low doorway,
our fontanelle, the trout's dimpled feet.

# THE FLITTING

'You wouldn't believe all this house has cost me—
in body-language terms, it has turned me upside down.'
I've been carried from one structure to the other
on a chair of human arms, and liked the feel
of being weightless, that fraternity of clothes. . . .
Now my own life hits me in the throat, the bumps
and cuts of the walls as telling
as the poreholes in strawberries, tomato seeds.
I cover them for safety with these Dutch girls
making lace, or leaning their almond faces
on their fingers with a mandolin, a dreamy
chapelled ease abreast this other turquoise-turbanned,
glancing over her shoulder with parted mouth.

She seems a garden escape in her unconscious
solidarity with darkness, clove-scented
as an orchid taking fifteen years to bloom,
and turning clockwise as the honeysuckle.
Who knows what importance
she attaches to the hours?
Her narrative secretes its own values, as mine might
if I painted the half of me that welcomes death
in a faggotted dress, in a peacock chair,

no falser biography than our casual talk
of losing a virginity, or taking a life, and
no less poignant if dying
should consist in more than waiting.

I postpone my immortality for my children,
little rock-roses, cushioned
in long-flowering sea-thrift and metrics,
lacking elemental memories:
I am well-earthed here as the digital clock,
its numbers flicking into place like overgrown farthings
on a bank where once a train
ploughed like an emperor living out a myth
through the cambered flesh of clover and wild carrot.

# THE HEIRESS

You say I should stay out of the low
fields; though my hands love dark,
I should creep till they are heart-shaped,
like Italian rooms no longer hurt by sun.

When I look at the striped marble of the glen,
I see the husbandry of a good spadesman,
lifting without injury, or making sure
where the furrow is this year the ridge
will be the next; and my pinched grain,
hanging like a window on the smooth spot
of a mountain, or a place for fawns, watches
your way with horses, your delicate Adam work.

But I am lighter of a son, through my slashed
sleeves the inner sleeves of purple keep remembering
the moment exactly, remembering the birth
of an heiress means the gobbling of land.

Dead leaves do not necessarily
fall; it is not coldness, but the tree itself
that bids them go, preventing their destruction.
So I walk along the beach, unruly, I drop
among my shrubbery of seaweed my black acorn buttons.

# Venus and the Rain

# ODE TO A POETESS

I

The rain has left a scare across the countryside;
the air at the bottom of the sky is swimming closely.
What survives of our garden is held together
by the influence of water, as if we could only live
in the shelter of each other, and just leave the matter
where we must leave all the doors that matter.
How clear and beautiful and hard to bear,
the shutters of these full delaying months,
like a window not made to open, or a house
that has been too long to let, my dark woman's
slope. While the noise of the moon is like
valerian drops when you come into a room
late at night, or the strangling of a river
to give shape to its fall. Half-real, half-dreamed,
untouched, untouchable, the yet-to-be-born weather,
distempering me as lips disturb the vespered worlds
of grapes, this onset of a poetess and her
persuasive bones sending me and my life away.

2

I will not write her name although I know it,
with the never-to-be-repeated awakening
of a letter's morning freshness, or the wide-
apart windows I recall of the summers of love,
where my scholar's fingers bungled their role.
Now you are in a poem of your own cold
making, on your second fret, your life knit
like a bird's, when amid the singing
of the Sparrow Hills you yourself could not sing.
It is ten o'clock, I am thinking of those
eyes of yours as of something just alighted
on the earth, the why that had to be in them.
What they ask of women is less their bed,
or an hour between two trains, than to be almost gone,
like the moon that turns her pages day by day,
letting the sunrise weigh up, not what they have seen,
but the light in which the garden, pressing out into
the landscape, drew it all the more into its heart.

# THE SITTING

My half-sister comes to me to be painted:
she is posing furtively, like a letter being
pushed under a door, making a tunnel with her
hands over her dull-rose dress. Yet her coppery
head is as bright as a net of lemons. I am
painting it hair by hair as if she had not
disowned it, or forsaken those unsparkling
eyes as blue may be sifted from the surface
of a cloud; and she questions my brisk
brushwork, the note of positive red
in the kissed mouth I have given her,
as a woman's touch makes curtains blossom
permanently in a house: she calls it
wishfulness, the failure of the tampering rain
to go right into the mountain, she prefers
my sea-studies, and will not sit for me
again, something half-opened, rarer
than railroads, a soiled red-letter day.

# AVIARY

Well may you question the degree of falsehood
in my round-the-house men's clothes, when I seem
cloaked for a journey, after just relearning to walk,
or turning a swarthy aspect like a cache-
enfant against all men. Some patterns have
a very long repeat, and this includes a rose
which has much in common with the rose
in your drawing, where you somehow put the garden
to rights. You call me aspen, tree of the woman's
tongue, but if my longer and longer sentences
prove me wholly female, I'd be persimmon,
and good kindling, to us both.
Remember
the overexcitement of mirrors, with their archways
lending depth, until my compact selvedge
frisks into a picot-edged valance, some
Swiss-fronted little shop? All this is as it
should be, the disguise until those clear red
bands of summerwood accommodate next
winter's tardy ghost, your difficult daughter.

I can hear already in my chambered pith
the hammers of pianos, their fastigiate notes

arranging a fine sightscreen for my nectary,
my trustful mop. And if you feel uncertain
whether pendent foliage mitigates the damage
done by snow, yet any wild bird would envy you
this aviary, whenever you free all the birds in me.

# ISBA SONG

Beyond the edge of the desk, the Victorian dark
inhabits childhood, youth-seeking, death-seeking,
bringing almost too much meaning to my life,
who might have been content with one storey
and the turned-outwards windows of the isba.*
Its mournful locus, I sit like a horse chosen
for its strength, requiring to be renamed
'Monplaisir', with my two hands free. I have heard
in it the sound of another woman's voice,
which I believed was the sound of my own,
the sound the first-timeness of things we remember
must make inside. And although she was eager
to divide her song, from her I took nothing
but the first syllable of her name, so the effect
was of a gentler terrain within a wilder one,
high-lying, hard, as wood might learn to understand
the borrowings of water, or pottery capitulate
its dry colours. Otherwise I might have well
ignored the ground that shone for me, that did enough
to make itself rebound from me, out of which I was made.

*Isba: Russian one-storey dwelling.

# HARVEST

I have taken you for granted like a house,
the harvest of your soft, stone smile. I have
made you come with me to smell, with your
winter beard, the treasure of the most sinful
oceans; or left you lunching at a Russian
hour, so that you might find my poem
wrinkled under your plate, like a beautiful
season you could never be prepared for.

I am the sky of a long day, working
out its twilight—how to make that steadily
impulsive blue taper off its solemn
rind, to fall like a sea-poem in shreds
between your fingers. Your hand takes it
with the strange whiteness prisoners let grow
over themselves, remembering the Florentine
light of restaurants, mourning their tables of rice.

Without ever saying to me you are tired
of the art of raining, with its oh-so-masculine
kisses, and the way it draws its suicidal
bloom across the wall like a huge long

painting of the sea. As if some blue god
denied September opening her doors so wide,
his sharp sound unanimous lest
twilight and I come at the same time.

# VENUS AND THE RAIN

White on white, I can never be viewed
against a heavy sky—my gibbous voice
passes from leaf to leaf, retelling the story
of its own provocative fractures, till
their facing coasts might almost fill each other
and they ask me in reply if I've
decided to stop trying to make diamonds.

On one occasion I rang like a bell
for a whole month, promising their torn edges
the birth of a new ocean (as all of us
who have hollow bodies tend to do at times).
What clues to distance could they have,
so self-excited by my sagging sea,
widening ten times faster than it really did?

Whatever rivers sawed their present lairs
through my lightest, still-warm rocks,
I told them they were only giving up
a sun for sun, that cruising moonships find
those icy domes relaxing, when they take her
rind to pieces, and a waterfall
unstitching itself down the front stairs.

# THE RISING OUT

My dream sister has gone into my blood
to kill the poet in me before Easter. Such
a tender visit, when I move my palaces,
the roots of my shadow almost split in two,
like the heartbeat of my own child, a little
blue crocus in the middle of a book, or the hesitant
beginning of a song I knew, a stone-song
too small for me, awaiting a drier music.

She gentles me by passing weatherly remarks
that hover over my skin with an expectant summer
irony, soliloquies that rise out of sleep,
and quite enjoy saying, 'Rather a poor year'.
I continue meanwhile working on my arm-long
'Venus Tying the Wings of Love', hoping
she will recede with all my heroes, dark
or fair, if my body can hold her bone to term.

For any that I loved, it was for their hair
that never really belonged to them, its colour
like a line of clouds just about to crumble,
the breaking of ice in a jar. In my mind,
I try and try to separate one Alice

from the other, by their manner of moving,
the familiar closing of the unseen room,
the importunate rhythm of flowers.

If she had died suddenly I would have heard
blood stretched on the frame, though her dream
is the same seed that lifted me out of my clothes
and carried me till it saw itself as fruit.

# HOTEL

I think the detectable difference
between winter and summer is a damsel
who requires saving, a heroine half-
asleep and measurably able to hear
but hard to see, like the spaces
between the birds when I turn
back to the sky for another empty feeling.

I would bestow on her a name
with a hundred meanings, all of them
secret, going their own way, as surely
as the silvery mosaic of the previous
week, building itself a sort of hotel
in her voice, to be used whenever
the tale was ruthlessly retold.

And let her learn from the sky, which was
clever and quiet, the rain for its suddenness,
that yes on its own can be a sign for silence,
even from that all-too-inviting mouth.

# DOVECOTE

I built my dovecote all from the same tree
to supplement the winter, and its wood
so widely ringed, alive with knots, reminded me
how a bow unstrung returns again to straight,
how seldom compound bows are truly sweet.

It's like being in a cloud that never rains,
the way they rise above the storm, and sleep
so bird-white in the sky, like day-old
infant roses, little unambitious roads,
islands not defecting, wanting to be rescued.

Since I liked their manners better than
the summer, I kept leaning to the boat-shaped
spirit of my house, whose every room
gives on to a garden, or a sea that knows
you cannot reproduce in your own shade.

Even to the wood of my sunflower chest,
or my kimono rack, I owed no older debt
than to the obligatory palette of the rain
that brought the soil back into tension on my slope
and the sea in, making me an island once again.

# FELICIA'S CAFÉ

Darkness falls short by an hour
of this summer's inhibitions:
only the cold carpet
that owns a kind of flower
feeds any farm or ocean
around the bedroom's heart.

Each day of brown perfection
may be colour enough for bees:
the part of my eye
that is not golden sees.

# LIME TREES IN WINTER, RETOUCHED

Black is my continuum, my black wheat ripens
from peach black, vine black, to the resins
of darkness. That is how good a picture
should be, oil abetting, light disturbing,
hoisted between two windows like the soul
of modesty, constantly straightening against them.

But I am agitated less by glass or apertures
than moisture trapped like a stain or white
secretion, an old swab I was confident
had broken down to paste, or was ingrained
in the next meconium, my intent and cherished waste.

# On Ballycastle Beach

# WHAT DOES 'EARLY' MEAN?

Happy house across the road,
my eighteen-inch deep study of you
is like a chair carried out into the garden
and back again because the grass is wet.

Yet I think winter has ended
privately in you, and lies in half-sleep,
or her last sleep, at the foot
of one of your mirrors—hence
the spring-day smile with which
you smarten up your mouth
into a retina of new roofs, new thoughts.

None of my doors has slammed
like that. Every sentence is the same
old workshop sentence, ending
rightly or wrongly in the ruins
of an evening spent in puzzling
over the meaning of six o'clock or seven:

Or why the house across the road
has such a moist-day sort of name,
evoking ships and their wind-blown ways.

# APPLE FLESH

The room getting lighter and darker
is a kind of travel also.
No dream could find its way in here,
up the now weak stairs,
where my body tasted like apple flesh
the day and night of fifteen countries,
or we sat about, unsmiling,
in a long, twisting sunset of 1910.

The thought of snow
clutched my face like a train
ducking clouds. I remembered
white pictures of birds and sun-healed
water—birds that had lost
their ability to shiver,
and died in the brainwashed sea.

Rock pulled away from rock
till the sea went out of its mind;
and my road in a sudden triangle
warned how the dreamer is in danger
when his dream begins, like that,
with the weather.

# SEA OR SKY?

Small doses, effleurage will do,
because I never garden. Wednesday comes
out of the rim of bones with a port-wine
stain on its face, a day of possible
excitements, no sky, yet you know immediately
the colour it should be. I play it down,
the agitated sky of my choice; I assume
that echo of light over there is the sun
improperly burning. In a sea of like mood
a wave is trying to break, to give a reason
for water striking something else, and the grey
below the wave is a darker version
of the moisture-laden sky I should be working in.
(Not the clear water of your sleep where you
seem lighter, and the garden's voice has gone inside.)

The athletic anatomy of waves, in their
reflectiveness, rebirth, means my new, especially
dense breasts can be touched, can be
uplifted from the island of burned skin
where my heart used to be, now I'm
seeing eyes that, sea or sky, have seen you.

# BLUE VASE

My overblouse is a garment made
for rest, work, movement. I permit
on my body only that which glides,
the roving ache of all shared things—
love, rest, and dreams.

My house is a small blue vase,
as difficult to give you as a present
from a trousseau or layette, being
held too tightly by my own
determined touch:

determined to steady your heart,
as a painting that gathers up
the light of some astonishing hair,
the rare dimming of a ship
early in the voyage.

Not losing his temper will come out
in one man's paintings of forty
of his dreams, his stair-step children,
as if he had studied all the dreams
dreamt in one night

with the same fierceness with which
we treat a fever. In the dream
that preceded the poem, I was standing
outside a house that had your face;
from opposite ends

re-chose you in my dream-speech,
without telling you or anyone what it meant:
to be the insouciance of the room,
interrupted, re-created—to be the innocence
you have just learned to say.

# THE BLUE SHE
# BRINGS WITH HER

*for Teresa*

November—like a man taking all
his shirts, and all his ties, little by little—
enters a million leaves, and that
lion-coloured house-number, the sun,
into his diary; with a rounded symbol—
*nothing*—to remind himself of callow apples,
dropping with a sense of rehearsal in June
as if their thought were being done by others.

The mirror bites into me as cloud into
the river-lip of a three-cornered lake
that when the moon is new is shaped
like the moon. With a sudden crash
my log falls to ashes, a wood of winter
colours I have never seen—blood-kissed,
the gold-patterned dishes
show themselves for a moment like wild creatures.

While any smoke that might be going loose
the hot room gathers like a mountain
putting out a mist, and not the kind that clears.
Something you add about mountains makes
my mouth water like a half-lifted cloud
I would choose, if I could, to restrain
as a stone keeps its memories.

Your eyes change colour as you move
and will not go into words. Their swanless
sky-curve holds like a conscious star
a promise from the wind about the blue
she brings with her. If beauty lives
by escaping and leaves a mark, your wrist
will have the mark of my fingers in the morning.

# FOUR O'CLOCK, SUMMER STREET

As a child cries, all over, I kept insisting
on robin's egg blue tiles about the fireplace,
which gives a room a kind of flying-heartedness.

Only that tiny slice of the house absorbed
my perfume—like a kiss sliding off into
a three-sided mirror—like a red-brown girl

in cuffless trousers we add to ourselves by looking.
She had the boy-girl body of a flower,
moving once and for all past the hermetic front door.

I knew she was drinking blue and it had dried
in her; she carried it wide awake in herself
ever after, and its music blew that other look

to bits. If what she hunted for could fit my eyes,
I would shine in the window of her blood like wine,
or perfume, or till nothing was left of me but listening.

# BALAKHANA

A town will never draw your mind to it
like a place where you have camped.
You will remember the very curve
of your wagon-track in the grass
where the ring swayed and was broken, almost,
as if someone had cried a message to you,
in one word, once, and would not repeat it.

Compare the most metallic of sounds,
the sound of elevators at night, or a car
stopping outside, a plane throwing herself
forward into space. The door I found
so difficult to close let in my first
European feeling which now blows about,
a cream-coloured blossom, with a blue vigour.

And if it were spring I would have sold
my leather jacket back to the short rains,
and folded, or unfolded, slowly
through all the burning hours of the day,
as if a giant upright cloud had been tied to me.

That flap of earth leaned against the sun
as women lean their faces to the wall

giving birth. Its mountains stretched
and spread and strangely took shape
from the smells that ran along them,
their deeply responsible pauses and heights
striking sphere after sphere of sparks.

Inside me everything was blurred
like tea with smoked milk, the stone
in the fruit, the meaning, the child
that left me no ground. As I stood
in thought by a window, I saw the glass-
clear sky above my head like solid
floorwork, become a sword half

out of its scabbard, and suddenly
filled like a glass with wine.
As if from its high site it too had drunk in
more than one stormy sunset, and more
than blood.

Things of the same kind are separated
only by time—I prayed the moon,
meant only for the moment,
would have it in him
to go on as beautifully as he had begun.

# HAREM TROUSERS

*for Nuala Ní Dhomhnaill*

Asleep on the coast I dream of the city.
A poem dreams of being written
without the pronoun 'I'.

The river bends lovingly
towards this one, or that one, or a third.
The staircase resumes its never-mentioned
ladder shape, as anything
that is being hurt overflows its innocence.

It straightens, stands, it walks
timid and incongruous
through roadblocks and breadlines.
It holds the hundred and first word
in its fingers and tears it apart,

so the openness within the sound
is forced to break, dislodging
its already dove-grey music.
An extreme and simple feeling
of 'What if I do enter?'—

As I run to fetch water
in my mouse-coloured sweater,
unkempt, hysterical, from
the river that lives outside me,
the bed whose dishevelment
does not enchant me.

Your room speaks of morning,
a stem, a verb, a rhyme,
from whose involuntary window one
may be expelled at any time,
as trying to control a dream
puts the just-completed light to rest.

# THE DREAM-LANGUAGE
# OF FERGUS

I

Your tongue has spent the night
in its dim sack as the shape of your foot
in its cave. Not the rudiment
of half a vanquished sound,
the excommunicated shadow of a name,
has rumpled the sheets of your mouth.


2

So Latin sleeps, they say, in Russian speech,
so one river inserted into another
becomes a leaping, glistening, splashed
and scattered alphabet
jutting out from the voice,
till what began as a dog's bark
ends with bronze, what began
with honey ends with ice;

as if an aeroplane in full flight
launched a second plane,
the sky is stabbed by their exits
and the mistaken meaning of each.

### 3

Conversation is as necessary
among these familiar campus trees
as the apartness of torches;
and if I am a threader
of double-stranded words, whose
*Quando* has grown into now,
no text can return the honey
in its path of light from a jar,
only a seed-fund, a pendulum,
pressing out the diasporic snow.

# ON BALLYCASTLE
# BEACH

*for my father*

If I found you wandering round the edge
of a French-born sea, when children
should be taken in by their parents,
I would read these words to you,
like a ship coming in to harbour,
as meaningless and full of meaning
as the homeless flow of life
from room to homesick room.

The words and you would fall asleep,
sheltering just beyond my reach
in a city that has vanished to regain
its language. My words are traps
through which you pick your way
from a damp March to an April date,
or a mid-August misstep; until enough winter
makes you throw your watch, the heartbeat
of everyone present, out into the snow.

My forbidden squares and your small circles
were a book that formed within you
in some pocket, so permanently distended,
that what does not face north faces east.
Your hand, dark as a cedar lane by nature,
grows more and more tired of the skidding light,
the hunched-up waves, and all the wet clothing,
toys and treasures of a late summer house.

Even the Atlantic has begun its breakdown
like a heavy mask thinned out scene after scene
in a more protected time—like one who has
gradually, unnoticed, lengthened her pre-wedding
dress. But, staring at the old escape and release
of the water's speech, faithless to the end,
your voice was the longest I heard in my mind,
although I had forgotten there could be such light.

FROM

# Marconi's
# Cottage

# TO CALL PAULA PAUL

*for Brenda McKeown*

Winter begins the way no one ever
moves. I have postponed her now
to Friday, till I have thrown
autumn's image on a
heap of smouldering leaves.

She did not arrive uninvited,
more than invited; her narrow
mouth pleased me, the ideas
inside it. I received her
in a sleeveless frock,
a significance above daylight,
a twin of April who might bring
a softer light to bear
on what the wind didn't dry.

Since she was water-shy, we
embraced only in doorways and on the sea-
wall, the safe balcony
with its frayed chairs, while
the heavy light lay solid,

golden, on the heavy, white sand.
At night she fell diagonally
into my bed like ripe
fruit, or a waterless river.

If you want to picture me,
I am lying full length, on my back,
as though a woman were carrying
me (this is my way of sleeping
off bad news), as though my soft,
pink, rented carpet were following
the music of my mother-to-be dreams,
keeping close to the walls, listening
with outstretched fingers as a bed never will.

In these discreeter lights, well satisfied
with rain and uncertainty, I dissect again
my Christmas cards for 1934, side by side
at their workless desks, a windowful of faces
slides away, and smells of emptiness,
like the breeze that forced itself
through a conspicuous eyelet in her dress.

I did nothing, I didn't cry;
I held the permanent bangle on her wrist

for a long time. In the bright July
my window seemed too big, all day
long to insult me, with its pale heaven,
putting supple hands around my throat.

Our hearts were all beating on
the far left, something was starting
at the top of her left breast,
to furnish it ironically. I touched
her foot with mine; also I shook
my head at the mirror, all
blotches and ripples, the dark
marks symmetrically dividing
up her face, as if from deep snow,
suddenly a sordid light
was sent up into a warm room.

The wind is at its cruellest at breakfast;
it has mouths, it outshouts me,
it knocks cameras out of newspapermen's
haphazard hands, it makes sure
books get torn during arguments.
In the film-like freedom
of its movement, it blows
the puppet clouds through a key.

Most children have theatre in them,
my one-child audience smiles
like a deck-chair unrelaxed, some
hoped-for person with too-white a face,
the blue-black hedge of her shadowless
eyes absorbing nothing of this different
light of seven o'clock in the morning,
the half-height curtains,
the house-lights left on.

I hear her voice like a telephone
torn from the wall by lightning
where she is telephoning endlessly.
The house is too pretty, the air
is tasteless, there are no seasons yet.

In the typewriter, very thin paper
is folded double—it has been
lifted out of the century.
The bloodless flowers draw
attention to her breast, where
I look for a little price tag
on that curious rustling 'R'
in my mornings.

So many orange skies have smashed
the light bulbs of the weather,
I look critically at the completely
missing week. If you are changing
trains by starlight, darling,
wear a white tie deluded by
a white shirt, for when I called
him 'bought', I only wounded him;
they're *his* soldiers, *his* lorries,
recruiting ghosts in your street tonight.

# JOURNAL INTIME

In the dreams of men the pattern
of the wallpaper by moonlight
is the death-devoted colour of masculinity.
And in artfully-placed mirrors,
a single, grieving shape, to the
weak-eyed, echoes and re-echoes,
more than sister, more than wife.

Red is the colour of art and of the
true centre of the summer
whose gestures endanger the carpet's
new nimbleness and heat, trapping
shadows, dissipating all the pauses
of the day and night. It is
a two-faced fruit, a lifelong winter.

I am a Platonic admirer of her
flowing, Watteau gowns, the volume
of Petrarch in her lap. It is so
unthinkable she should look outward
from the depressed, pink light of her
one-time nursery, if only to dilate
upon the same two faces, if only, upon the snow.

In a child's first (and most satisfying)
house, where everyone is repeated
in everyone else, the door that is so light
to her, so dark to us, is wise enough
to dream through. Her voice fills the mouth
of her own mirror, as if she were a failure:
as if, what is lifelike, could be true.

# A SMALL PIECE
# OF WOOD

On the secret shelves of weather,
with its few rhymes, in a pause
of blood, I closed the top
of my lesson-filled inkwell,
a she-thing called a poetess,
Yeoman of the Month.

In pale frock and raspberry
boots, my waist the circumference
of no more than two oranges,
I rode out to hunt, with my
white linen eyes and my lips
cut out of a piece of red material.

On my left two rivers flowed
together without mingling,
as though someone had unrolled
two different ribbons side by side,
or three-quarters of the sky, allowed
to touch, but not to mix, with winter.

The sweepings of my study
seemed all spoiled remnants
in which the colour had run,
as if the hook of a clasp
had got from eyelet to eyelet
till it could unbuckle no further.

Pictures in children's books used
to be painted in by children,
each with a silent pen, a guide,
seated round a table, each a colour
to himself, wherever it appeared,
no one child a whole picture.

While my numberless blues
have neither end nor beginning,
arranged like a tribe of lovers
in a circle—my headdress
a flaxen wig, a velvet bandeau,
a beaver hat, with a plume of feathers

dropped from the neck and breast
of a black-winged stilt:
every apple is a feather-room
for seed's infectious star, and every man
who calls a woman 'Choorka',
for a hundred and eight ruled pages.

# GIGOT SLEEVES

There are bibles left about the house:
here is the bible open, here is the bible shut,
a spreading here, a condensation there.

The double-cherry performs a dance behind
triple gauze, she takes out the bulldogs,
masters a pistol, sleeps on a camp bed

without a fireplace or curtain, in the
narrow sliproom over the front hall—
a woman-sized, un-beringed, inexact fit.

When she hears the wheels of his carriage
she blows out the candle, she does not yearn
for the company of even a lamp.

For a gown-length, she chooses
a book-muslin patterned with lilac
thunder and lightning. Her skirts

are splashed with purple suns, the sleeves
set in as they used to be fifteen years
ago. If she takes up a piece of sewing,

she will be shirt-making; in a laundry-book
she writes as though fifteen hundred Englishmen
had been slaughtered just beyond the garden,

or it was there Trelawney threw the frankincense
and salt into the fire, poured the wine
and oil over the wave-worn depths of Shelley.

Her petticoats have neither curve nor wave
in them, the whole depth of the house,
like a secret tie between a wound and its weapon.

And everything is emaciated—the desk
on her knees, the square of carpet, the black
horsehair sofa—and the five-foot-seven by sixteen

inches, of a pair of months, stopped.

# THE MOST
# EMILY OF ALL

When you dream wood I dream water.
When you dream boards, or cupboard,
I dream a lake of rain, a race sprung
from the sea. If you call out 'house' to me
and I answer 'library', you answer me
by the very terms of your asking,
as a sentence clings tighter
because it makes no sense.

Your light hat with the dark band
keeps turning up; you pull it right
down over your head and run the fingers
of your right hand up and down
in a groove on the door panel. A finger
going like this into my closed hand
feels how my line of life turns back
upon itself, in the kind of twilight
before the moon is seen.

A verse from a poem by Lermentov
continually goes round

in my head. A full ten days
has elapsed since I started my
'You can go or stay' letter, increasingly
without lips like the moon that night,
a repercussive mouth made for nothing,
and used for nothing.
Just let me moisten your dreamwork
with the lower half of the letter,
till my clove-brown eyes beget a taller blue.

# NO STREETS,
# NO NUMBERS

*for Janice Fitzpatrick*

The wind bruises the curtains' jay-blue stripes
like an unsold fruit or a child who writes
its first word. The rain tonight in my hair
runs a firm, unmuscular hand over something
sand-ribbed and troubled, a desolation
that could erase all memory of warmth
from the patch of vegetation where torchlight
has fallen. The thought that I might miss
even a second of real rain is like the simple
double knock of the stains of birth and death,
two men back to back carrying furniture
from a room on one side of the street
to a room on the other. And the weather
is a girl with woman's eyes like a knife-wound
in her head. Such is a woman's very deep
violation as a woman; not like talk,
not like footsteps; already a life crystallises
round it; and time, that is so often only a word,

'Later, later', spills year into year like three days'
post, or the drawing-room with the wall
pulled down.

I look into the endless settees
of the talk-dried drawing-room where all
the colours are wrong. Is that because
I unshaded all the lamps so their sunny,
unhurt movements would be the colour
of emotions which have no adventures?
But I'm afraid of the morning most,
which stands like a chance of life
on a shelf, or a ruby velvet dress,
cut to the middle of the back,
that can be held on the shoulder by a diamond lizard.
A stone is nearly a perfect secret, always
by itself, though it touches so much, shielding
its heart beyond its strong curtain of ribs
with its arm. Not that I want you
to tell me what you have not told anyone:
how your narrow house propped up window
after window, while the light sank and sank;
why your edges, though they shine,
no longer grip precisely like other people;
how sometimes the house won, and sometimes

the sea-coloured, sea-clear dress,
made new from one over a hundred years old,
that foamed away the true break
in the year, leaving the house
masterless and flagless. That dream
of a too early body undamaged
and beautiful, head smashed to pulp,
still grows in my breakfast cup;
it used up the sore red of the applebox,
it nibbled at the fortnight of our violent
Christmas like a centenarian fir tree.

I talk as if the evenings had been fine,
the roof of my shelves not broken
like an oath on crossed rods,
or I had not glimpsed myself
as the Ides of September, white
at the telephone. Two sounds
spin together and fight for sleep
between the bed and the floor,
an uneasy clicking-to of unsorted
dawn-blue plates, the friction
of a skirt of hands refusing to let go.
And how am I to break into
this other life, this small eyebrow,
six inches off mine, which has been

blown from my life like the most aerial
of birds? If the summer that never burnt,
and began two days ago, is ashes now,
autumn's backbone will have the pallor
of the snowdrop, the shape of the stone
showing in the wall. Our first summer-time
night, we will sit out drinking
on the pavement of Bird Street,
where we kissed in the snow, as the day
after a dream in which one really was
in love teases out the voice reserved for children.

# THE UNPLAYED ROSALIND

*for Anne Devlin*

July presides, light with a boy's hat,
dressed in black with his feet on a cushion,
his voice-print is too dry for the stage.

The long-stemmed flowers comparatively
rained, and the tumultuous sea was making me
sterile, as though a hand from within it
slowly drove me back, we were small objects
on its edge.

The telegraph pole sang because a horseshoe
brushed its foot, and a spider's web darkened
on my finger like a kiss that has to be paid
with the veil lowered, a sweet-sour kiss through tight-
bitten lips that could make me drunk.

I have lived on a war footing and slept
on the blue revolution of my sword;
given the perfect narrative nature of blue,
I have been the poet of women and consequently
of the young; if you burned my letters
in the soiled autumn they would form two hearts.

The room which I thought the most beautiful
in the world, and never showed to anyone,
is a rose-red room, a roseate chamber.
It lacks two windowpanes and has no waterjug.
There is red ink in the inkwell.

Upstairs above my head lives someone
who repeats my movements with her double
weeping. My heart beats as though it were
hers, and sometimes I have her within my clothes
like a blouse fastened with a strap.

She moved in her dream, she lost her dream,
she stretched her arms and tossed her head
as a river burrows its bed till the bed burns.
Her dress reminded me of curtains torn
like a page from a bedroom window.

There was a rustle in the lock of the door,
a noise like grasshoppers as though a great
moth were caught in it. Then the door
simply waved, and a long white sheet
of paper came gliding from under it,
like a coaster shoved beneath everyone's
wineglass, or glass being cut under water.

In her there was something of me which
he touched, when she lay on his arm like the unknown
echo of the word I wanted to hear
only from his mouth; she spoke words to him
I had already heard.

She said, 'This is too bright for me',
preferring to see the fire-red rip down heaven
as a saucer of iced water where she could
dip her hands, as in the reciprocal blue
ashes of his eyes.

She kissed him as if he were her child
like a gull rubbing its beak against
a jagged window, and my body felt
all its gossip's knots being traced.

She removed the rose from my mouth
like the taste of fruit or a button left
on the top of a cupboard. Though she swore
that she did not carry
another man's child under her heart,
my seed is a loose stormcoat
of gold silk, with wide sleeves, in her uterus.

# THE PARTNERS' DESK

Yesterday was a gift, a copy of the afternoon,
a heavily wrapped book, a rolled manuscript.
Its paper was buff with blue lines, the sheets
ragged at the top, and not quite legal size.
It was secured on three sides by green ribbons
like a wooden tongue of land or the leafy miles
of a ribbon-maker and, whether it was a letter
he withheld from me, I swore to seal it through death.

The colour is deep enough by itself to make
the children pray for the dead; it is a children's morning.
I arranged the Christmas tree in its green outfit,
producing its green against the grey sky like handwriting
that has been traced over or, when snow tires us,
the sunshine inside and out of my birthday dove.
Both our birthdays are today, and I was playing with
its feather on the bed as if it were a brake

on the thawing weather, that almost-summer
had already arrived. Being still in the grip
of a dream of pearls which robbed me
of my un-English language (yesterday
he dreamed of laburnums). It is his December,

though the wine is May's, and we should keep birds
only in winter, as we burn the winter
in our curse-laden, extinguished Christmas tree.

Everything I do passes through a narrow door,
and the door seems rather heavy. When I play
the piano my eyes turn brown; it is not a matter
of eyes, it is something darker than eye-colour,
and we are all part of it. When I teach the continents
to my favourite daughter, my father is there
though I do not see him. His mood is towards evening.
He asks the bird how many years he has to live,

or how long the hours will continue to strike.
How very deliberately the bird breaks off,
praising the stillness. He compares this cry
with his outward appearance, he strokes the veins
on the back of his left hand and extends
his fingers, he looks up at the ceiling
and down at the floor, he feels in his breast
pocket and pulls a green pamphlet out,

saying, 'The finest summer I can ever remember
produced you,' and I remember a second,
gentler dream, of my wedding year,
where we took a walk across loose stones,

and he took my hands and stretched them out
as if I were on a cross, but not being punished.
You know the renewed rousing of your fingers
in a dream, your hand glides through the air,

they are not fingers at all. He will leave me
the school clock, the partners' desk, the hanging
lamp, the head bearing the limbs, as I will leave her
the moonphase watch and the bud vase. I restart
my diary and reconstruct the days. I look upon
the life-bringing cloud as cardboard
and no reason for the life of another soul, yet still
today is the true midsummer day.

# OPEN ROSE

The moon is my second face, her long cycle
still locked away. I feel rain
like a tried-on dress, I clutch it
like a book to my body.

His head is there when I work,
it signs my letters with a question-mark;
his hands reach for me like rationed air.
Day by day I let him go

till I become a woman, or even less,
an incompletely furnished house
that came from a different century
where I am a guest at my own childhood.

I have grown inside words
into a state of unbornness,
an open rose on all sides
has spoken as far as it can.

# BREAKING THE BLUE

Deluged with the dustless air, unspeaking likeness:
you, who were the spaces between words in the act of reading,
a colour sewn on to colour, break the blue.

Single version of my mind deflected off my body,
side-altar, sacramental, tasting-table, leaf to my
emptying shell, heart with its aortic opening,

your mouth, my dress was the scene that framed
your shut eye like hands or hair, we coiled
in the lifelong snake of sleep, we poised together

against the crevice formed by death's forefinger
and thumb, where her shoulder splits when desire
goes further than the sender will allow.

Womb-encased and ever-present mystery without
release, your even-coloured foliage seems a town garden
to my inaccessible, severely mineral world.

Fragments of once-achieved meaning, ready to leave
the flesh, re-integrate as lover, mother, words
that overwhelm me: You utter, become music, are played.

# OVAL OF A GIRL

The summers of our house peel and rot.
Sunset has begotten them, thinking he could shut
it in with varnish. But one discarnate shadow
can be worth a whole generation; I am flooded
by no ocean but a second you.

Who might just as well have been water
breaking and mending with a dark little movement,
a kind of forlorn frenzy leaking over into sound,
for whose unpronounceable blue I am an ear,
alerted, stretching, not as I had prayed.

I have a hundred ways of turning
this year of the world's redemption
into an ominous nativity, a face too fast
and fallen, too formed and fresh to seem asleep,
already soiled by this eye-opening winter.

Near-child, much-needed, present tense,
your first grown-up spring is under wordless control,
beyond poetry, like a poem of the deepest calm
never to be written, or a city re-beguiled
by useless fields that were all but air to me.

# MARCONI'S COTTAGE

Small and watchful as a lighthouse,
a pure clear place of no particular childhood,
it is as if the sea had spoken in you
and then the words had dried.

Bitten and fostered by the sea
and by the British spring,
there seems only this one way of happening,
and a poem to prove it has happened.

Now I am close enough, I open my arms
to your castle-thick walls, I must learn
to use your wildness when I lock and unlock
your door weaker than kisses.

Maybe you are a god of sorts,
or a human star, lasting in spite of us
like a note propped against a bowl of flowers,
or a red shirt to wear against light blue.

The bed of your mind has weathered
books of love, you are all I have gathered
to me of otherness; the worn glisten
of your flesh is relearned and reloved.

Another unstructured, unmarried, unfinished
summer, slips its unclenched weather
into my winter poems, cheating time
and blood of their timelessness.

Let me have you for what we call
forever, the deeper opposite of a picture,
your leaves, the part of you
that the sea first talked to.

# ON HER SECOND BIRTHDAY

*for Emer Mary Charlotte Rose*

In the beginning I was no more
than a rising and falling mist
you could see through without seeing.

A flame burnt up the paper
on which my gold was written,
the wind like a soul
seeking to be born
carried off half
of what I was able to say.

It seems as though
to explain the shape of the world
we must fall apart,
throw ourselves upon the world,
slip away from ourselves
through the world's inner road,
whose atoms make us weary.

Suddenly ever more lost
between the trees
I saw the edge of the forest
which had no end,
which I came dangerously close
to accepting for my life,

and followed with my eye a shadow
floating from horizon to horizon
which I mistook for my own.
It grew greater while I grew less,
gliding like a world, a tapestry
one looks at from the back.

The more it changed
the more it changed me into itself,
till I regarded it as more real
than all else, more ardent
than love. Higher than the air
of a dream,
a field in which I ripened
from an unmoving, continually nascent
light into pure light.

My contours can still
just be made out, in the areas of fragrance

of its power over me.
A slight tremor betrays
the imperfection of the union
in its first surface.

But I flow outwards till I am something
belonging to it and flower again
more perfectly everywhere present in it.
It believes in me,
it cannot do without me,
I know its name:
one day it will pass my mind into its body.

FROM

# Captain
# Lavender

# LINES FOR
# THANKSGIVING

Two floors, their invisible staircase
crouching muscularly,
an old wall, unusually high,
interwoven like the materials for a nest,
the airtight sensation of slates:
all as gracefully apart
as a calvary from a crib
or the woman born in my sleep
from the stranger me that is satisfied
by any street with the solemn name of a saint.

The moon there, fuller than any other,
slips through my fingers into every fold
of the sky in turn, stirring up satin
like a mother roughing a boy's hair.
Eternally repeating its double journey
and the same message, as if it were
still impossible to speak
from one town to the next.

The fire keeping in all night
is an extra gas jet, its several

thicknesses unequal in length
like the rays of a monstrance.
If I had just won a victory
it was over everything that was not
myself, by the water's edge.

# DANTE'S OWN DAY

I wanted to hold him only as cotton
holds sweat, a sub-sea, birth-green river
of eggs in a private nest of smell.

The struggles of a series of intertwisted minds,
arranged by no mind, one on top of another,
in a growing ribbon of warmth.

Not to be lived in, a shell may need to be
too sturdy, stretching backward from the unwritten
part of angel, that unhealthy tissue
around the moment.

An acorn of a blind, denuded, unbegun,
unsheltered and unfinished, draws across a floor
on the mortal side of language,

a leaf detaching itself
from the narrative 'tree'
attempts to seal its meaning.

Then the voice that supplied the story
will be a character rounded-off outside it,
writing itself into those fumbling breaks
through which desire is completely trained:
bound in the bed like an account book.

# ELEGY FOR AN IRISH SPEAKER

Numbered day,
night only just beginning,
be born very slowly, stay
with me, impossible to name.

Do I know you, Miss Death,
by your warrant, your heroine's head
pinned against my hero's shoulder?
The seraphim are as cold
to each other in Paradise:
and the room of a dying man
is open to everyone.
The knitting together of your two spines
is another woman
reminding of a wife, his life
surrounds you as a sun,
consumes your light.

Are you waiting to be fertilized,
dynamic death, by his dark company?
To be warmed in your wretched

overnight lodgings
by his kind words and small talk
and powerful movements?
He breaks away from your womb
to talk to me,
he speaks so with my consciousness
and not with words, he's in danger
of becoming a poetess.

Roaming root of multiple meanings,
he shouts himself out
in your narrow amphora,
your tasteless, because immortal, wine.
The instant of recognition
is unsweet to him, scarecrow word
sealed up, second half
of a poetic simile lost somewhere.

Most foreign and cherished reader,
I cannot live without
your trans-sense language,
the living furrow of your spoken words
that plough up time.
Instead of the real past
with its deep roots,
I have yesterday,

I have minutes when
you burn up the past
with your raspberry-coloured farewell
that shears the air. Bypassing
everything, even your frozen body,
with your full death, the no-road-back
of your speaking flesh.

# THE AISLING HAT

October—you took away my biography—
I am grateful to you, you offer me gifts
for which I have still no need.

I search for a lost, unknown song
in a street as long as a night,
stamped with my own surname.

A spy-glass at the end of it,
a cool tunnel crushed by binoculars
into your grandfather's house.

The elegant structure of the heart
is a net cast over everything in sight,
its lace design of perforations, truancy.

Over your face a cognac eagleskin
was tightly stretched, my cart-horse,
dray-horse, drew your heavy chariot

chasing after time you beat aloud
which had already vanished into overtones:
you were his co-discoverer, his museum,

his clock of coal, clock of limestone,
shale or schist, his mountain top
sculpted into a foal, his warm pitcher.

Even your least movement was connected
with the very composition of the soil,
you lived and died according to its laws.

Your Promethean head radiated
ash-blue quartz, your blue-black hair
some feathered, Paleolithic arrowhead,

set off the bold strokes of your ungainly
arms, created for handshakes, sliding
like the knight's move, to the side.

You were intoxicated like a woman
caressed with the lips alone
by the noise of your thousand breaths.

You felt nauseated, like a pregnant
woman, a rose inscribed in stone,
unread newspapers clattered in your hands.

Your horse-sweat was the poetry
of collective breathing, your urine-colour
the sense of the start of a race.

Your eyebrows arched like a composer's,
an accordion of wrinkles repaired
the fluids of your forehead, then drew apart.

Your powerful thorax gave velvet-
throated orders, there was a married charm
in your nuptial animation floating forward

to sow itself in the arid
frontier atmosphere. Your skin changed
to an absolute courtesy

but never ceased dreaming;
seeds of laughter pierced your chest
that now lies ensconced in the velvet.

Broken sign of the unbroken continuum,
you fused into a single thread,
time fed you with lightnings and downpours

so you rained hushing sounds,
while river air hovered over the room
and sucked in a crescent of the sea.

You sharpened yourself like a pencil
in the tender midwife of your shell,
in your geometric giddiness.

Your golden hands like hills
of tired rags stirred up the dust,
flushed horseman, streaked feldspar.

There was fire in your hands, blisters
on your palms as if you had been rowing,
heavy fire in your naked eyes

monkish in their furious, yellowish
glitter, still and sensual the shining
points of your equine eyes.

Twin wings unseverable
were those enormous eyes, legs of the heron
reconciled to their uselessness.

Neck of the swan theatrically
open, ripping off the days due to you,
expressing your allegiance.

A noose around the icy place
from which flowed your consciousness
like mineral-water cheeriness.

The earth like some great brown
ceiling came rushing at your head.
No one heard it hiss in the shadows.

Roses which must have been cut
in the morning stood exchanging lights,
as your phonetic light turned off

and the lips of your fireproof eye
burned like poppies, firmly reminding
everyone that speech is work.

Until we remembered that to speak
is to be forever on the road,
listening for the foreigner's footstep.

I felt a shiver of novelty
as if someone had summoned you
by name, to the most beautiful applause.

Your eye raised the picture
to its own level, you retreated
into the picture before my eyes

like hello or goodbye;
I got tangled up in it
as in a robe ready to be woven

from a soft *L* and a short aspiration,
or the most recent barbaric layer
the bark of linden peels off itself.

Woodcutting tuned you, absorptive
and resorptive, to an entire segmented
lemon grove of fatigue and secret energy.

You burst the frontier at some
undefended silk crack—shreds
of splashed brain on the chestnut trees.

Now all questions and answers rotate about—
did it thunder or not? Now I begin
the second stage of restoring the picture.

The helix of my ear takes on new whorls,
becomes a bittersweet instrument,
to undress spring from the neurotic May,

the inherited river, the world
which, unpopulated, continues
to signal his speech-preparatory moves.

He does not resemble a man
waiting for a rendezvous.
The area he covers in his stroll

is too large, he is still
a stranger there, until his storm matures,
and what might have been alive, knowledge-bearing.

His body is unwashed, his beard
wild, his fingernails broken,
his ears deaf from the silence.

Carefree skater on air, his language
cannot be worn down, though I
avoid it in my feebleness.

He controls my hair, my fingernails,
he swallows my saliva, so accustomed
is he to the thought that I am here.

I need to get to know his bones,
the deep sea origins of the mountains,
the capsule of his crypt,

how life below starts to play
with phosphorus and magnesium.
How cancelled benevolence gains a script

from a departure so in keeping
with its own structure—his denial
of history's death, by the birth of his storm.

# FLIRTING WITH SAVIOURS

It did not look as if anybody lived there,
rebellious sea on both sides of a narrow town.
Nature was a backdrop that had to be defended,
nothing could land at night, its night was so perfect.

Folded world of fierce under-winds that cried
eye-catching kisses most speakingly; basin
of enlaced hands, forensically linked
or fettered to the undecaying moon.

In our gentle meetings wrath did not seize them,
but the elements paused, without greatly moving air,
a kind of false or treasonable sunlight,
where something frightening that happened was fixed forever.

No nourishment other than chemicals.
Partly idyllic stoppage of time
that made the criminal fit the crime,
not rooted there but hazard-banished,
ruled out like the fear of being afraid.

Betrayers sent to guard, burnt wine,
outnumbered only by the one missing face;
outbreak of history better than no catastrophe ever.

Stored statelessness, hereafter glimpses,
surfaces to which gold could be applied, worse than saints—
men utterly outside themselves, with the taint of women.

# THE OVER MOTHER

In the sealed hotel men are handled
as if they were furniture, and passion
exhausts itself at the mouth. Play kisses
stir the circuits of the underloved body
to an ever-resurrection, a never-had tenderness
that dies inside me.

My cleverly dead and vertical audience,
words fly out from your climate of unexpectation
in leaky, shallowised night letters—
what you has spoken?

I keep seeing birds
that could be you when you stretch out
like a syllable and look to me
as if I could give you wings.

# THE ALBERT CHAIN

Like an accomplished terrorist, the fruit hangs
from the end of a dead stem, under a tree
riddled with holes like a sieve. Breath smelling
of cinnamon retires into its dream to die there.
Fresh air blows in, morning breaks, then the mists
close in; a rivulet of burning air
pumps up the cinders from their roots,
but will not straighten in two radiant months
the twisted forest. Warm as a stable,
close to the surface of my mind,
the wild cat lies in the suppleness of life,
half-stripped of its skin, and in the square
beyond, a squirrel stoned to death
has come to rest on a lime tree.

I am going back into war, like a house
I knew when I was young: I am inside,
a thin sunshine, a night within a night,
getting used to the chalk and clay and bats
swarming in the roof. Like a dead man
attached to the soil which covers him,
I have fallen where no judgment can touch me,
its discoloured rubble has swallowed me up.

For ever and ever, I go back into myself:
I was born in little pieces, like specks of dust,
only an eye that looks in all directions can see me.
I am learning my country all over again,
how every inch of soil has been paid for
by the life of a man, the funerals of the poor.

I met someone I believed to be on the side
of the butchers, who said with tears, 'This
is too much.' I saw you nailed to a dry rock,
drawing after you under the earth the blue fringe
of the sea, and you cried out 'Don't move!'
as if you were already damned. You are muzzled
and muted, like a cannon improvised from an iron
pipe. You write to me generally at nightfall,
careful of your hands, bruised against bars:
already, in the prime of life, you belong
to the history of my country, incapable
in this summer of treason, of deliberate treason,
charming death away with the rhythm of your arm.

As if one part of you were coming to the rescue
of the other, across the highest part of the sky,
in your memory of the straight road flying past,
I uncovered your feet as a small refuge,
damp as winter kisses in the street,

or frost-voluptuous cider over
a fire of cuttings from the vine.
Whoever goes near you is isolated
by a double row of candles. I could escape
from any other prison but my own
unjust pursuit of justice
that turns one sort of poetry into another.

# THE WAR DEGREE

You smell of time as a Bible smells of thumbs,
a bank of earth alive with mahogany-coloured
flowers—not time elaborately thrown away,
(you wound yourself so thoroughly into life),
but time outside of time, new pain, new secret,
that I must re-fall in love with the shadow
of your soul, drumming at the back of my skull.

Tonight, when the treaty moves all tongues,
I want to take the night out of you,
the sweet Irish tongue in which
death spoke and happiness wrote:

a wartime, heart-stained autumn drove
fierce half-bricks into the hedges; tree-muffled
streets vanished in the lack of news.
Like a transfusion made direct from arm
to arm, birds call uselessly to each other
in the sub-acid, wintry present. The pursed-up
fragrances of self-fertile herbs
hug defeat like a very future lover.

Now it is my name and not my number
that is nobody now, walking on a demolished
floor, where dreams have no moral.
And the door-kiss is night meeting night.

# CAPTAIN LAVENDER

Night-hours. The edge of a fuller moon
waits among the interlocking patterns
of a flier's sky.

Sperm names, ovum names, push inside
each other. We are half-taught
our real names, from other lives.

Emphasise your eyes. Be my flare-
path, my uncold begetter,
my air-minded bird-sense.

# Shelmalier

# SCRIPT FOR AN UNCHANGING VOICE

Here is a stone with a stone's mouth inside,
a shell in which a lighter shell has died,

one with a honey bullet in its heart,
one that has lain full-length from the start.

The leaves are tongues whose years of blood are locked
in the wrong house, time feels unclocked

or has been dead too long by now to cast
its freshly slaughtered shadow from the past . . .

# DREAM IN A TRAIN

The world shovels snow
into a pond without an echo.
This image of water made visible
is a cry as warm as life.

The house is a perfect body
surpassing, unwriting me,
as the density of black repairs
light, even grows it.

Some part of my pine-wooded
mind sleeping or dead
was a tightened-up light
I was sheltering for years

which destroy something other
than flowers, eluding
by means of their own surface
the unchanging sea

around a swimmer
whose sigh is a fold
imposed upon the waves,
suggestive of an awakening.

# THE FEASTDAY
# OF PEACE

Deep in time's turnings
and the overcrowded soil,
too familiar to be seen,
the long, long dead
steer with their warmed breath
my unislanded dreams.

View-thirsting at the wound-open
window, their weighted bending
down from a beclouded
day in the real past
runs a kind of springtime
through the air we will breathe.

Their lace-curtain Irish
anchoring the moon-lines
along the twisted sea-coast
chafes like a boat
in a sky-voyage the English
meaning so unlike language.

As summer's funeral
in the deceitful wane of the war
is like a paper bride
in an unwomanly room
touching her mildly widowed
newlywed body—

so these puritan fields
that could not give the answer
when the whole key of childhood
spoke like an eye—
were death fore-experienced
though the leaves were all there.

# CIRCLE WITH FULL STOP

Birds are the only creatures who can feel
two things at once. I see and hear nothing
but the cheesemonger and chandler,
I've lain in the shallow dents where
sleep breaks all day with a pistol
by me, when I could have been swimming
under fire across the Danube.

But to bring out the taste of the month
I've had my dive into your head
where it was summer till three-thirty
and always afternoon.
In the dance of the months I was August,
now I've gone back into winter clothes,
a March sea, the glacial white of the reading-room.

I am pinning together a chair-cover
from the flaring fragments of your shirt,
drawing my hands to and from my lips
like dusk adding truth to the chain
of pictures lining the house.
When sleep flings its inkstand, everything
is a few degrees clearer.

# THE POTTER

To my word spouse
I was not Eve nor Helen,
not Mary nor Sophia,
but the fool of the house.

He followed my breath
and left it in the face
of one who was pronounced dead
by the history of faith.

I sit in the lotus
of courtly love,
in the locked dialogue
of errors outlived

and deny that he is
all spices commingled,
with my entire body sown,
deny that he is light.

# FROM THE
# WEATHER-WOMAN

Not even a dead letter
a pseudohope from your pseudohome.

You are dissolved in me
like the death of the century.

I need your summer movements
as the spirit needs the world,

my non-world the inner
gospel of your letters.

From the unhardened nature
of the memories, your prison

look, that mood, that number,
leads a road where nothing

can unhappen, to the meeting
of two opennesses: the one

I write before the visit,
the one you will write after it.

# SELF-PORTRAIT IN
# THE ACT OF PAINTING
# A SELF-PORTRAIT

Unreadable day, you must have sat
too often by the dying. Cracked window,
of no property, you must have heard
the busy tinkle of blood.
Never youthful light,
with the minimum of heat,
you collar whole walls
in the feel of trampled flower-ness,
you traverse the city from end to end
in the sky's safety,
to an outer position of a double
circle of positions,
where her Musehood has withdrawn
into a single drop.

The striped gown she lifts
without the painting looking
is the edgeless gunboat surface
on which we all exist.

Each dusting scrapes an internal winter
from her summer missal, like self-caressing,
long-folded clothes, of a sailor
home from sea.
And no answering of seige
but her ears closed and her lifetime's gaze,
the forced glint of a real pupil
through the inferior blue,
on her own reflection, undigested,
in the fruit with their dismembered trunks
of faces.

# STONE WITH
# POTENT FIGURE

My inward country slept
an oak south of the third furrow,
giving the wild bees
sugar from her fingers
in their shy approaches to communion
with her coaxing hands.

The wind blew in circles
through the isles of the trees
as it will under a mountain,
painting the pivot counties
grey in grey as independent
as dependent men.

Her head to the west,
her legs to the east,
her black-stained left arm bent;
the waist front of her skirt
a very clumsy seam along
the slightly constitutional fields.

Beneath her a frond of bracken,
the wings of six jackdaws
and two crows, twelve small wings
and four large, three
crab apples on the breast
over her light-loving heart.

There was a fall of semi-pure
earth, but the lid fitted
so tightly, not a speck of soil
had worked its way within,
only a little heather, moss,
a birch leaf at the root end.

Her bones were reduced to a pale
blue powder that the dried muscles
held like thongs; her grave
no more than a low
unworkable bank
of cultivated disbelieving.

That she herself was buried
weaponless in her coffin
in that summertime I know
from the flowering head of yarrow
laid with care by her right knee—
carpenter's or soldier's wort, a cure for possession.

# THE SOCIETY
# OF THE BOMB

The sleep of her lover is her sleep:
it warms her and brings her out to people
like half-making love or the wider now,
exceptionally sunlit spring.

Before violence was actually offered
to us, we followed a trail of words
into the daylight, those palest and clearest
blues, and all the snow to come.

# MANTILLA

*for Shane Murphy*

My resurrective verses shed people
and reinforced each summer.
I saw their time as my own time,
I said, this day will penetrate
those other days, using a thorn
to remove a thorn in the harness
of my mind where anyone's touch
stemmed my dreams.
                          From below
to above all decay I stated
my contentless name and held
the taste as though it were dying
all over true in the one day light.


My sound world was a vassal state,
a tightly bonded lattice of water
sealed with cunning to rear
the bridge of breathing.
                          And my raw
mouth a non-key of spring, a cousin
sometimes source, my signature
vibrational as parish flowers.

# The Soldiers
# of Year II

# HELEN'S WAR

Bertie finished early. He was nineteen when he returned from the training college at Strawberry Hill. There was a job going in the local school in Glenshesk, and you'd think they would have given it to him, eldest of twelve children, parents lifetime parishioners, but no, Pat Duffin got it and your father I'm sure was brighter than him. But that's the way of the world and it didn't do him much good in the end, for he died within a few years of T.B. All Bertie could get was subbing jobs, in Loughgiel and Magherahoney—Mrs McCollum that just died across the road, her uncle was the principal. They were very fond of him in Magherahoney.

Then there was one Sunday Bertie and I were at Mass, and just putting our pennies on the plate, and the priest asked how he was doing, and Bertie was able to say to him, he'd just been offered a permanent post in Belfast. He didn't know how to take this, and I couldn't help adding: 'I don't see why you couldn't have given him the job here, father, and saved him going all that way from home.' It was shortly after that I took sick, and maybe it had something to do with talking back to a priest. I was only twenty three then, and was on my back for three years.

Bertie went to the city for the first time on October 1st, 1942. The Thursday before he died he was up here, and in good form, except at one point he looked serious and commented: 'It's fifty years ago to the day, Helen, that I first set foot in Belfast.' He had bad digs, most of the time, though one woman he stayed with was from Ballycastle, and treated him well. He had a violin left to him, and it disappeared somehow with all the moves. On July 6th, 1943, I was brought to Foster Green Hospital in Belfast by taxi. We went out for a drink before I left but I wasn't able for it. They put you over while they inserted a tube to draw the fluid off the lungs, and you had to lie completely flat with it, or it came out; and once it came out with me, and they didn't put me over putting it back in again, only brandy and that, I'll never forget it, so I swore I wouldn't move again, and I didn't for three years.

Bertie was evacuated to Saul in County Down with the schoolchildren, but he still visited every Sunday and often during the week as well. He had different girls but he never brought your mother up. There were people dying all the time round me but I wouldn't die *for* them. It wasn't that I was strong, I just had this will to live. Then they took me to the Royal to do the operation, and Bertie gave blood for it. I have no ribs on this side, they took them all away to cut the lung out, or most of it. But there was still fluid in what remained. We got St Anne's ointment and Lourdes water, but there was no penicillin available for they needed it all for the soldiers. Then one day in 1946 they brought in this wee bottle of stuff over from England that cost about £800, and the next week I was able to go home.

You know how when you've got used to a place, or institutionalised, you don't want to leave. Bertie came with me on the train, and I didn't know where I was, I couldn't make anything out, everything was strange to me. They were all there except Margaret, and that spoiled the day for me, for she was already ill, and died the following March in the big snow.

Your mother didn't bring you up much on account of it. Once I wanted to take you down the lane to the haunted house, the fairies' house, we would have had a great day, but she wouldn't let me take you through the grass in case you got your feet wet. We were just setting off, when she gave this cry, or shriek, from the gate, and so we had to turn back.

# LIFE AS A
# LITERARY CONVICT

I have experienced a wilderness
printed black on white.
Tarnished years of silver fever.
All my minds are weapons.

I miss the tunic of rain that settled in
like an old heart complaint,
the polluted air so bracing,
the great non-meetings
wrapped up in politics.

Signs of the still recent war
creep among the people like a plague,
dressed as Phoebus.
While I wander about in search of the dead,
all I see are the living,
being pulled into full existence,
emerging as if from a cellar.

Everything that ended in gunshots
and news of massacres

and third-class funerals that smelled
of nothing, pressed out of my reader's eye
the last tears of childhood.

Ceilings were lowered and gardens
obliterated, the deaf and the absent-
minded were being shot,
but the clockwork life of the unchanging
street, and the uninterrupted houses in rows
neutralised the lava of war
to a normal part of winter
at an enormous cost.

Fresh families pose like birds
in the wound-up spring, healing
at a distance in a slower time.
The roughneck soldier that fell
in a flooded field has managed to create
a republic without republicans.

He lies in his English envelope
like the Greek word for Greekness,
defender of Throne and Altar,
while the frontier is guarded
by the small wombs of two chickens.

# REVIVAL OF
# GATHERED SCENTS

Someone will tap a door
with just a single finger,
while beaks are still tucked under wings,

and the woman nestling
close to the blinds
has received a letter in the dark:

a knotted letter, snow-moistened,
the ink-seal on the outside frozen.
She tries to unfasten the rice-paste,

her sleep-swollen eyes aching
at the ink extremely dark
in some places, light in others.

The paper white as a flower
wraps up a single petal of mountain rose,
whose dead white head remains

alone in the fields. It cannot
withstand the autumn's strength
with a cheap prayer,

expecting too many years.
The house is one where no one
cares about the gate,

and for a time the pond
stays as it was, the entire garden
is the same green colour,

and the two stars seem
closer than usual, fern on the tiles.
Now she has carefully scented a robe

of glossed silk, beaten and stretched,
with a pattern of decaying wood
and chrysanthemums faded in part

at the hems; yet she seems
perfectly clad, high-kneeling
to the God of Leaves

at the small half-shutters,
at the very edge of roofs.
Because the tree pear-skinned,

streaked with rain,
is divided into a thousand branches
full of curved promises

whose leaves do not change.
How depressing when there is
no reply poem, no return poem

written on a fan with three
ribs! No next morning letter
attached to a spray of clover

with a long iris root enclosed,
clear-toned as the face a child
has drawn on a melon.

# LOVE AFFAIR
# WITH FIREARMS

From behind the moon boys' graves
bleed endlessly; from photograph
to browning photograph they blacken
headlines, stranded outside of time
at the story's frigid edge.

Though they are long buried
in French soil, we are still speaking
of trenches, of who rose, who fell,
who merely hung on. The morning drills
secretly, like an element that absorbs.

We are right back where we were
before the world turned over,
the dreary steeples of Fermanagh and Tyrone
are all that Sunday means. Their North
was not 'The North that never was'.

Artemis, protector of virgins, shovels up
fresh pain with the newly-wed

long-stemmed roses, pressing two worlds
like a wedding kiss upon another Margaret:
lip-Irish and an old family ring.

It's like asking for grey
when that colour is not recognised,
or changes colour from friend to friend.
I track the muse through subwoods, curse
the roads, but cannot write the kiss.

# THE CHIMNEY BOYS

It is late earlier. The faded biscuit-pink
of the infill building inflames the edge
of the slanted blue and white chessboard.

Those darling policemen, we thought,
but no, they really were insurgents,
a swatch of crumbs of colour going dark.

Every room has a soul if it can be prised
open, a little shy of its own beauty,
under the feudal right of introspecting houses.

But those who saw them skylarking
in the gutters, looking clean and wholesome,
were unable to find any text to discredit it.

Factory children, valued as little as rabbits,
or decaying birds transfixed on a dog-spear,
small gentry, urchins in dreary gambols,

they were climbing boys, boys of the best size,
little boys for soot-caked flues,
seeds of sleep harvesting the dew

on what was left of Saturday, for an ideal
Sabbath. A pewful of children throbbing
for liberty, a bundle of jointed sticks,

lashed from their beds clutching their clothes
over their arms by loving Sabbatarian
engines purifying their manhood.

A boy is hard to quench, mingled
too much with bitter wood; but what is a toasted
child, lying in his negritude,

his corkscrew motion, his sable consolation,
to a deranged dinner party? Murder by proxy,
a melancholy but imperious necessity.

Four assorted clergy, bigot and crank,
with scriptural thrust and parry ready
to add their own enemies to theirs,

pin the bosoms of their lutestring shirts
back, as if they had saved as many
lives as Marconi, normal persons,

six-pounders spraying glass marbles
and clay balls. Soon there would be brooches
for sale with 'God over, curse Great Britain'.

Then the vulture, emblem of time,
calling the hour by another name,
will lay sunflowers at their feet on the longest day.

# FILMING THE FAMINE

I

My meal of pleasure crisped like a wave
in the perfect circle of his lips,
not helped by the winds and the air:

the primal garment of his skin,
and the brush-braid on the hem of his voice,
was an answer as soft as the question.

It was an evening made of cold clouds
and the necessary flight of natural sleep,
which takes the malice of memory into the half-world.

Springs that had carried the steely dusk
only hours old into my heart
lost their coral heartbeat and were still.

The island glittered like some silver and crimson
winter fruit. The river's small leaden blue
pulse was only sad as one is in a dream.

Its whistled lament took blood from cattle
and brought down birds—its scarlet cross-stitch
roped me into grudging prayer. . . .


2


The image of peace was superimposed
on a sea composed of fragments,
fairground notes like a fragile line of surf
came from the stamens of her pearly fingers,
out of the shelter of her veil,
into the shadow of her arms.
She was all stranger, like some war
that had escaped out of a book,
all but Irish, fought according
to the code of the angels.

Mass paths and other useless roads,
devastated by street battles,
and soldiers impersonating soldiers
overlapped in a film presentation
of an island that had lived through
two famines, and still comes into my dreams.

Brickmakers and coal-heavers
and people without end
slid together in a cell of false time,
a summer of sorrow,
flat lines of darker black
in the sunken inkpots
of the brig Eliza Ann,
The Intrepid, the ship Carrick,
Hebron, Erin's Queen, Syrius,
Virginius, The Sisters,
Elizabeth and Sarah.

The springing forms of her hands
were a merciless screen against sight:
but if the notes were high and opened heaven—
they might suddenly hear something.

# BLUE KASINA

I

You walk as if you are kissing the earth
(she is breathing—why not me?),
or tapping a page like a drum, you invite
the bell of my hardly used breasts to sound.

My second breast imbibes your graces,
the mind-river of my very first love,
which lets the leaves pass through
as when he wanted my face to be more stricken.

You march your breastless body
back and forth with all its volumes
like a frontier, still agitated
by piety, blood beneath your everyday verdure:

as the semi-divine womb is able
to move around in search of moisture,
and will find it in an opening between two arms,
a path slit as if for letters.

2

I am sight-singing you, music
made out of music, listening to the unfamiliar
mass of your male womb and robust hymen,
your someoneness, paid not to undress.

I am just this much inside your breath
all by itself where you die into
the tide of each unique breath
as the full language watering your mouth

with flow lines of water, their colourlessness
almost intense. The drop of my dress
into the pool of my dress is a brown garland,
a fresh crown, that has never been so closed before.

And for seventeen minutes I brighten
by watching like rarely observable
starsets how your thoughts end,
greeting your rust in whatever rings and shines.

3

The glassed subconcious of the city
is overwhelmingly sweetened, the narrowness
of the light is false, the shadows false,
draping the window cushions with gold watches.

So now each soldier has swallowed a draught
of *eau-de-vie* in which the flag's
ashes have been dissolved, we can
begin again with the 'A' names

in the wood-book, using the soot of wood.
It is a kind of confusion of faithfulness,
this unkind holding of the torch of wishlessness,
that turns gently within my unmet gaze

an afterkey not turned far enough
to snag and soften all about it
the regrowth on the cleared table
whose threading would give, mile by mile.

# A RELIGION
# OF WRITING

The island's lock weakened
as in dreams; the sea beauty
of the air was moved
by warmed music which caused
that question to vanish.

Dreams as common as rain
returning to the outdoors
one whom the earth has reclaimed
in the passage from the name
to the body, the remoteness
of name to meaning.

Despite the thicket, the writing
is set low, half-empty lines
with ivy leaves and fruits
acting as punctuation.
Such unsteady capitals,

the backward S, the L
with its foot slanting sharply

downwards, the B with detached
loops, a G consisting of two opposing
curves, a Q with its extended tail

taken up inside, a long palm-like
Y. There are cuts reinforcing
the heads and the forking
of the uprights, letters of smaller
size placed inside others.
Winged death with two conversing
skeletons, a flame
with no clothing,
a death's head carved
with a human head inside it.

# AT MULLAGHMORE

Earth's memories in the natural dyes
of curtains half-fitted to each other.
There was a deep today
in their different starting-points
as if non-being thought
it had somehow got the better of being.

To love the world of that hour
was to hear the weather forecast
for a day already lived through
siding with the hurricane
whose presence or absence was the same.

The islands hung together
through the tasteless water.
Though something stayed back
and did the telling
every one of us
was the one who remained.

# DRAWING BALLERINAS

We are the focus of storms and scissor-steps.
A young girl that dressed up as a woman
and pulled her gown tight across her breast
now pays men to dance with her, as we would tie
the leaves to the trees and the trees to the forest.

A ringlet of hair tied with black silk
rests in a medallion of white shell, a machine-gun
in its nest, a crease in the middle of a flower.
The hair describes a protecting curve, a repetition
that is a completion, a dip in a mountain.

And the lines' desire is to warp to accommodate
a body, a lost and emptied memory of a lost
body, the virgin mind emptied from or of it,
to discover the architecture of pressed-together
thighs, or lips that half-belong to a face.

The body turns in, restless, on itself, in
a womb of sleep, an image of isolated sleep.
It turns over, reveals opposing versions of itself,
one arm broken abruptly at elbow and wrist,
the other wrenched downwards by the force of the turning.

It settles under its own weight, like some weighty
nude. It flattens to the surface on which it lies,
a series of fluid, looping rhythms, let loose
by one last feeling. As if it had obligingly
arranged its legs, or joined those imprisoning arms.

The oval of the head is a wire folded
in tension to spring back at right angles
across the neck from which it has been lifted.
And what are those unnerving sparks of matter,
the astonishingly open, misaligned eyes?

That suffer like a camera, and fall asleep
a great deal to subdue the disquieting
existence of others—an aerated grey, but
the page stays light, the paper with ease, at ease,
possesses the entirety of the sheets they occupy.

The contours become brittle and start
to fracture, as if the body-burden with
its stripped-down beauty, having rested,
removed her necklace, had put her gown
back on, tied back her hair, resettled her hat.

So that underlaid whiteness is reunified
by light into a breathing white, an undivided

whiteness, a give or take of space
across or within that same whiteness, that
simplest of solutions, the same whiteness everywhere.

This poem was written to commemorate Ann Frances Owens, schoolfellow
and neighbour, who lost her life in the Abercorn Café explosion, 1972. The
French painter, Matisse, when asked how he managed to survive World
War II artistically, replied that he spent the worst years 'drawing ballerinas'.

# THE COLONY ROOM

If you are touching, you are also being touched:
if I place my hands in prayer, palm to palm,
I give your hands new meaning, your left hand calm.

You define my body with the centre of your hand;
I hear through the shingled roof of your skin
your ear-shaped body enter the curved floor-line
of my skin. My hands just skim the cushioned opening,
the glitter of your mouth; all woods, roots and flowers
scent and stretch the map that covers your body.

Less touchable than the birth or continuation
of Ireland, in its railed enclosure, your root-note,
in its sexual climate, your kingdom-come eyes,
year-long, inactive lover, durable as paradise.

Like small shocks in the winter, neck to neck,
the mirrors reflected the coloured ray
the evenings needed most, when the day . . .
asked for night in that mistletoe way.

# THE MINIVER

Another black date, black gondolas
absorbing the blue, trying to renew
our appetite for war like half-a-cake
eaten by a catfish, or a coconut
carved into a fool's head.

Even the most war-weary marauders
at the hour the century was born
were timing Christmas by the light
on their swords, galloping in every ceiling
into the ceiling of a cooler sky.

It was the hand of God at its purest
set the weapons cabinet with its fine holes
deep into the English brown and green earth
of the very lagoon, making use of heaven
to bind His blues with His own ultramarine.

And fettered Mars, so women looked away
from him as black stone, the colour of their thoughts,
so wine flowed from the statue
of sleep-inducing Mercury, a whole raft
of meanings on the inside of their lids.

This brittle peace, a palm's breadth in length,
is always morning, has that morning glitter,
gives the ever-narrower interior a feeling
of being outside, lines the walls with leather,
crushes the marble floor with her floss petticoat.

She is hope's brother, though the two people
inside her add up to less than a whole:
she is so placid, clean and fresh,
the rhythms of her warrior father invade other colours
than the lilac of her vase-room flesh.

# GAELTACHT
# NA FUISEOIGE

*New Year's Day, 1997*

Cubes of sky-wielded silence
yellow the light: the light
that would be glad
to bathe itself in you.

When for years I have months,
and my soul chimes
like an inhabited word,
a thinking which sucks

its substance, barer now,
enticing meaning, laying
word against word
like pairs of people,

broods in the wound,
an admitted infection,
the highroad's central
greatest ought.

The title refers to the Irish-speaking area of the Lapwing, which was part of
the Republican H-Block in Belfast's Maze Prison.

# HAZEL LAVERY, THE GREEN COAT, 1926

Agreed image, of your open self, your personhood,
do not put me into a sadness like your own,
though I am using your heated body with its
easy mark of beauty, its narrow grip on a segment
of the abstract world, for some clues.

He has been able to bring your inner sun
to full view, a real heartbeat and a lucid mind
inhabiting a body degrading into matter:
like a rosary made of plum stones, built *en
colombage*, your hospitality towards death

is the light of my own country. The lamp
without oil in your spine a hand-made candle
to light me to bed. Your sense of chastity
starts a shape in me attached to life at all
four corners, saying what your beauty means to you.

A wave heaping itself to feast like a plant
on much of what flames in my eyes, the world
of speech, a world that seems bared of its covering,
and has not a bone in its body. You are walking
within a tulip, and a fire of sea-coal in your house

not yet numbered leaves a blue path through
the warm cinder of your head. You throw a veil
of sinewy deception, of half-grown leaves,
over your eyes, walking up Air Street that moon-
ark body you had so often laid down. . . .

so that the living seem to go to bed
with the dead, most seasonably, a boy hobbles
with a log at his foot to kiss the bell-handle
of your lodgings: his most used words inking
that wintry mantle of aged snow, floating

in the middle of the unstitched page. You have
what used to be called a military bearing,
which is that of a child asleep on a cross,
the whitish patina of verdigris and rose
carmethian that begging soldiers forge

on the eight hanging days, as their ivory ticket
to the damaged sky where heaven tries to see itself.
And it is as though you actually wore armour,
with nineteen horses killed under you, seated upon clouds,
your seas unsailed since his blood fell directly

into the unfixed horizon.

# The Face of the Earth

# THE BROOD-BIRD

My encircler, I am placing a lock
upon my lips, though nine deaths
were in my unhemmed mouth
or thy mouth breast-white to my breast.

The tongue and knot and pulsing oil
of death without death goes round
in a thread, so I see neither the black
nor the white, tonight, in the upper chamber:

only the knee-woman, the world-woman,
the woman of songs.

# THE FACE OF
# THE EARTH

Now his private breath,
so easily pacified,
is in many ways an almost ideal
face, I have drowned in him
and his small elm coffin
of the English kind
keeps my vision in.

Our perfect and unmarked closeness
is a strangeness
that has made me sleepless
under a swarm of stars
turning the world into this world,
how it is what it is,
that it is what it is.

He was a bird which is not
in the habit
of sleeping on the sea—
not a sea-bird or river-bird—

a land-bird.
But no man killed by the sea
ever looked like that.

I caught myself reaching up
to his ear in whispers,
off the face of the earth,
in the field of the telescope:
I was afraid I could not
make a sound, that neither
of us was ever to hear
each other's natural voice.

I could not feel him,
and I did not know him
in his choice of that untempted
life, to bring his eyes nearer
to the mystery.

A deep ship moved
under his feet as she lay
cleared for sea, and slept,
her darkened sails
loaded with dew.

A flower showed
a little sail in the image
of the wind, dividing that moment
from the hour and the last flowers
we should see for the next
three months:

I am going to look
for land breezes
till the summer
when I should be whole again
to make his lungs consent
to draw air.

# THE WORSHIP
# OF THE PLOUGH

Only old women like the colour
of deep water, when the body is thrown
into a running stream and becomes
the ghost of a childless person.

A coil of twigs brushing out
the sowing basket, like fluid opium
into a catch-basin, as soon as possible
before noon, before the rice flower forms,

drives the water full into
that absolutely level field,
a field left vacant in me,
well-white and smooth.

I go to the field by night,
to the place where the earth begins
to become moist, to a piece
of moist earth stamped and injured

by rain, like an animal black
on the shoulders. The helpless seed
is as much as can be carried
under the arm, the grain as much

as two hands can hold.
And if it is the bright half
of the month, time is a word
formed from action, measured

in Credos, or Pater Nosters,
an Ave Maria said aloud,
a Miserere. A plough is slightly
passed over the field, in a circle,

from corner to corner, and first light
waters the field's pulse
to its supposed extremities,
a hedge of brambles not fixed

in the ground. When the first
leaf shows, the overburnt blisters
give out little shoots which
weaken it a thread-breadth,

then a finger-breadth, till it is
two-thirds grown. In the marriage
of a grove to a well,
or a well to an image,

trees look their best,
half-wearing the produce
of one field less desired
if you weed your fields in me.

# NAVICELLA

A sunken street, air over ice—
how could the earth be jealous of the air?
Of movement and an open road?

Only your wings have survived,
a few dark openings,
your face in semi-shadow,

the pure gold or azure of the window
partially filled in
with dusted red ochre.

Flower between two abysses,
prisoner of your own image, or any wartime,
your head is somewhat difficult to read:

age-old, unconsummated
emblem of charity, only ever young,
which of these worlds is ours?

Your angels seem to listen
to what they are playing,
and can be readily imagined

passing in and out of doors.
There is a strong sense that the dark
doorway on the other side of the courtyard

truly leads into an interior.
Despite the number of words lavished
upon you, I would have to wear out

the word 'perhaps', because there is
no other way than studying
the wax and honey of your face

for hours while the sun progressed
from east to west, the blue straps
of your bible, your billowy mauve cloak,

the absence of punchwork in your halo,
your gestures set ominously to 'dead'.
Something else is always awakened

by the annulment of time
sweeping through the universe,
developing plans for travel,

his bewitching performance
making a Roman journey,
the harshness of his touch

stretching out his arm
in a powerful diagonal thrust,
by which he desanctified the world

in the snowfall of August 358.
A moment after being touched
by the golden spines of his crown,

all of these people were healed
by his shadow, that is no longer
a blue or golden void,

a rood screen, of eucharistic grapes,
but snowgrace,
healing with its shadow.

# IMAGE OF
# MIGRATORY CRANES

Thus they go past one another
in the adultery of the heart,
with the bravado of addressing light,
that chill on the unjust soul.

Falling somehow out of love
with the glorification of voluntary death,
one could talk about one's long walks,
seeing no harm, in the same breath.

Love songs are always a dreary flight,
which will not be love, the word
wearing thin and hymnic;
yet because I feel how much a word,

I often try to forget, Jean Paul,
the homily of your earlier self,
like gods that are really believed in,
your river-poems, driven out of the bud.

For eight important years,
years that will really count,
I will choose a new kind of agitation
that will not be one great grave,

but will not be unbeseeming
to the gothic study where you appear
sparingly, nowhere more, and never
thus, amongst everything used.

# HIGH ALTITUDE LAVENDER

When snow fell for six hours
in an unforeseen direction,
the winter of fruit skins
recovered the footlight glow
of the sun as solid silver.

A gothic bouquet
of bronze-coloured roses,
standing up in military elegance
shackled to a trance,
flexed gleaming silken arches.

A stem of body-bound
orchids on a breathless postcard
changed their florid despair
to a midnight-blue glance,
and accepted to speak about next year.

A sheaf of country dahlias
in a communal ward

turned their humbled palms out
with morbid homage to embrace
the rustle of live wings.

I kept colliding with the absence
of my own heavy family,
fiery as this year's grapes
that the dew considered heartless,
as though they had grown deafer;

and addressed a conversation
to no one among us,
to the gardens framed by your windows,
that can imitate the shape of flowers
with their mere mouth and their empty fingers.

# VALENTINE NOT
# TO BE OPENED

As into young sleeps old rain washes
with its lovely assault, trees in February
cry out with a kind of relaxing
for remembrance or prayer, inclining to the earth.

The art of spring is a bloodless affair,
always romantic to us, never to itself;
light burns so heavy it loses colour
but seems to want to be there,

to be coaxed out, like a mind within flesh
to flesh without mind. Our rye field
that was mortgaged (my kitchen
I think I called it) omits the season.

Even the farmhouse is without windows,
and no cloud nests in it. The cup from which
I drank is unnumbered bits
of a bigger story, smeared by my lips.

Let me arrange that pillow in your own words
you wrote with that spirit pen, to make
your exit easier, including the arms you held
above your head as you were breathing out,

or deep stroke the waist of your foot
with some almost contemporary touch,
incursion of the road into the field,
misenveloped wayfaring tree.

# CHRISTMAS EVE SKY

On a day that cannot be anticipated,
half in the present and half in the past,
a rapid casting back of todays into yesterdays
is all that tells us we are seeing a path
through trees with a hill in the distance.

The sea, a strip of blue, aerated water,
receives its colour from the angles of two clouds
into its interior, as sanctuary and treasure trove,
all its feeling of open air, all equally lost,
like a star whose travels one wants to record.

My hand made a shining journey of its own
to its flowerlike, petalled head, too well kept,
whose resemblance is love, trued off with a knife,
its triple purity of fruit and glass already quite
radiant, rejoining the house that sparked it.

# HESTERNA ROSA

Still has become already,
and yesterday's rose
a red dove, swept away
with a leaf whisk.

The sundial's shadow
falls on nine
with the calmest gesture,
each in its utmost force.

Our city-music
was the singing of a Mass
for the relief of fever,
prefiguring the day

a small landscape
would be fashioned
from your hair's soul-circuit
under glass.

The cool womb
of your body-harp
and the moon as we
begin to see it

in the time-zone of evening;
the moon's voice
meets this moon within you,
brilliant as a forest

around the dusky nightmare
of the house, where the musicians
are being forced to play
death more sweetly.

# SHE IS IN THE PAST, SHE HAS THIS GRACE

My mother looks at her watch,
as if to look back over the curve
of her life, her slackening rhythms:
nobody can know her, how she lost herself
evening after evening in that after,
her hourly feelings, the repetition,
delay and failure of her labour
of mourning. The steps space themselves
out, the steps pass, in the mists
and hesitations of the summer,
and within a space which is doubled
one of us has passed through the other,
though one must count oneself three,
to figure out which of us
has let herself be traversed.

Nothing advances, we don't move,
we don't address one another.
I haven't opened my mouth
except for one remark,

and what remark was that?
A word which appeases the menace
of time in us, reading as if
I were stripping the words
of their ever-mortal high meaning.

She is in dark light, or an openness
that leads to a darkness,
embedded in the wall
her mono-landscape
stays facing the sea
and the harbour activity,
her sea-conscience being ground up
with the smooth time of the deep,
her mourning silhouetted against
the splendour of the sea
which is now to your left,
as violent as it is distant
from all aggressive powers
or any embassies.

And she actively dreams
in the very long ending of this moment,
she is back in her lapping marshes,
still walking with the infinite

step of a prisoner, that former dimension
in which her gaze spreads itself
as a stroke without regarding you,
making you lower your own gaze.

Who will be there,
at that moment, beside her,
when time becomes sacred,
and her voice becomes an opera,
and the solitude is removed
from her body, as if my hand
had been held in some invisible place?

# Had I
# a Thousand
# Lives

# READING IN
# A LIBRARY

You wake me up with the name
I carry inside me like a first
language. It becomes needles
on your lips, slightly grey, a waste
of light I swallow like a syrup.

A tree forks at the level
of your eyes, it spreads my dark
dipthong upward like a cup,
I place myself expectantly
under your open hand.

You talk with your hands
like two people, you zigzag
softly from person to person,
rubbing my names together
as if that were your goal,

not pushing my thoughts into
the space beneath the bed.
I bring a sentence to your body,
brimming like an island, I sit
filled with that, as with a bible.

# THE DEADEST
# DEATHS ARE
# THE BEST

—MONTAIGNE

You lay, grey and quiet,
herded into a ring,
by the exploded tree,
comely as a church,
but it was I who was
nailed there firmly.

The pool through its artifice
paints Narcissus.
His arms mark
the beginning of an embrace,
an embrace that is
only a splash.

But you, my more divine
brother, you have received
a thousand times

what I yearn to have
just once: hoarfrost
to your harsher sister,

snow, that other brightness,
that slides from the world
like a river, its
ardour of self-bestowing
a flaming evidence
of wild delight, like sunlight.

The diminished promise
of your voice becomes
illegible; image and spectre,
now framed,
snake within each other.
The washed sharpsand

with supposedly gold stars
saving your name plaque from Lethe,
yet draws within me
from outside,
infinite either way,
the aisleless horizon.

# THE PYX SLEEPER

Now where sensuousness begins
the air enjoys him, his open-air heart,
his open-eyed dream, his sexless sex.

What he is to me is to me
all that he is, he is for me
what he alone can ever be for me.

I delight without envy in his form,
his imparted self, the hidden and assured
oxygen and salt of my existence.

The new and ever newer water,
not the sterile baptismal water,
is the image of his eye, his natural mirror.

But why does his reflection
already want to wound me?
I know that he will still be the one

who someday takes my inward broken life,
but neither would I wish
that my soul be scattered.

There is nothing that makes passion
less transparent than the passionless
light, its miracles of anger,

receiving the rejected nature
into his heart again. We have a world
between us, exactly a world, and the nothing

out of which the world came
is nothing without the world.
I take hold of the purely thinkable

body with my lips closed, unclosed,
as if there were a rune less divine
that could make him mine.

# THE SLEEP CURE

The sea is the act of wiping,
a thought unhesitatingly
pointing into a sign.
A loving mouth bursts through it
like a natural gate.

When death floods a rasping
sweetness into the room,
you always feel yourself
to be much stronger,
you lock up the sea

far from your own life
in the mocking indoors of dreams
whose silence you have basely,
coarsely reached for,
whose neck you could wring.

Persons or streets
who give nothing but themselves
imitate the nothingness
of a bed that overtakes
each movement that our body sketches out

and vanishes spring-smelling
behind a wooden screen
till all that is left
of even the scent of melancholy
is the sky counting

in different sheets
of mauve transparent paper,
with my inward April
a number within it
alone with the boatman.

# FORCING MUSIC
# TO SPEAK

*And the napkin, which was about his head,*
*not lying with the linen cloths, but rolled up*
*in a place by itself.* —JOHN 20

*for Eamonn Whelan*


I love a church of lanterns
and narrative windows,
the light of old churches . . .

the shell of the bride of Christ
stains a universe whose gravity
is too weak to wrap its space around

until it joins up with itself,
using the patterns of goddesses
to carve with snow-knives a rain animal,

a lily of the valley, not
of the heights. Much to my awakening,
the illness spirits come close,

but I have no ear for their whispering:
the essence of their ghostliness,
shapes ten miles in time

that fail to reach eternal life
and have to buy each day.
To the east, a young man,

like a doll pruned from a live tree,
a female birch, standing on the corner
of a wall of the building,

thanks Radegund for her gift of chestnuts,
admires the graceful, sculpted cut
of Agnes' fingers, of which he finds a print

in the butter rising to the top of the milk
she sent him. Tree of music.
Like grass when greenness flows into it.

Greenest stem scenting all dry spices,
standing leafy in his nobility
as dawn breaks, his feet glowing like the dawn

through her secret, among the living rafters.
We cannot see his eyes, and can discern
only a hint of his mouth,

but this is where he stood,
his signature included,
delivering his body, his whirling,

musical body, musical glove, to the music
he knew in the sky.
A harp adorned with strings lies across his body,

in his chest, and answers to every touch.
A white cloud by his mouth,
he stands on a platform left by ruins

from the eighteenth century,
before diving into the early nineteenth:
a moment in which his head

is cast in shadow and his lower body melts,
his face bowed suspended,
though his inner strength beats from his heart

like a face. He has flung himself
as from a pier, featherweight,
vertical, post-human, resonant,

he is without a body,
broken in two by his fall,
paraded to the real places

free of all body, his breath
giving out before his song.
His lifeblood

a scarlet flood of sound
with something dark and thirsty about it,
it perishes much too soon,

and states this lack clearly,
the brilliance of the voice
altogether used up.

A shock wounds his windpipe,
one is too dark, the other splits his throat,
liable to rend from within.

But at the smallest particles of dust
his slit throat resounds,
like womb-wheat or a guitar of God,

his severed head continues to sing
as it floats down the Heber
and is immersed in stagnant winter water

to land on the island of Lesbos.
Winnowed and purged and stellified—
true forge embroidered in gold and writing—

I don't want,
I don't want you
to rest in the leisure times of the cosmos:

for we do not sing 'Requiem'
for such a soul,
but the 'Gaudeamus' Mass.

# The Book
# of the
# Angel

# THE PUBLISHER
# OF INWARDNESS

This is the time after seasons.
It is too warm for spruce
to sketch a deep horizon.

I photograph asleep
like the detachable soul of a child
the final resting place of metals

in the receiving waters,
so mobile in soil,
by my wordwork,

by taking his lifetime
into my mouth as a word
to make a world.

A word that ends up under
sea-ice, or a parable
by the seashore embroidering dawn.

# THE DREAM
# THEATRE

First I drew in the air the roads
like clouds thrown further back
and a heart like the sky:

then, in the sand, composed
of tiny starlike fragments of coral,
your story, in pieces, as it is.

A story of dreaming, sleeping
with one side of your brain
in the italicized darkness

that roams the world imagining
a world without empire,
lost and dangerous as a dream.

*

In the outline of your dream
you turn your head to the right,
but look to the left,

your mouth a little open as if
to bite, but never attacking thin air;
with real smiles changing its fine

structure, like the dreams
of a champion oyster, whose face
is then utterly forgotten.


   *


It had broken as it should have,
my sea-horse shaped memory,
the warm-blooded bowl of your sleep

without touching your brain,
building up its library
in its graveyard of dreams,

or your eight-day-old memories
that are paths into your dreams,
and your empty, high-quality waking.


   *


Until, note against note,
a dream comes on, and becomes
a place to live,

a dream-play in the open loop
of our dreams, now and equal,
white and coloured,

writing out the sleep debt,
a hundred minutes of dreaming,
underneath that late, inner star.

# FOUR VOICES WITHOUT AN INSTRUMENT

Another March month has come
to raise the temperature of the world,
a self-opening, clear, in mourning,
becoming light.

The northeast wind
reads the quarters of the sky
where the moon falls awake
into its own mouth
till day and night are equal.

There is no dust, no deluge.
The blue of the city has swollen
or returned to itself
in its dark ship
the reverberating sea.

Even the light, I thought,
like a bell in the air

already out of tune
through a slight snowfall,
would never be allowed its brightness.

Yet since we have been a conversation,
the three-in-one sign
of your stained-glass voice
has become my chosen one,
a garden surrounded by other gardens,
housing the seasons.

Though our lives may have overlapped
the musicians that blew out their candles
and left the stage, one by one,
now blow for me
a sunburst of winds
on their lowest strings;

so that not without wings,
when the mist vanishes,
the brightening, endangered earth
is the year's first angel.

# ARMED DANCE

I held in the same hand
male and female stones:
one blue variety giving
sweet light
like the sea close to shore;

and my increasing
certainty of touch
feared the virtue
of this weathered world
might be lost—

the personification
of the calm sea
and the soundful,
soul-tightening ocean,
might sever earth

from world,
though the god sealed them:
earth, the original ark,
holding his body
in its distant embrace,

the sky a prolongation,
and even an organ,
the colour of watered wine,
of earth missing water,
of his limping heart.

But it is not just any world,
despite the purposeless rain
these twelve April nights
ordered as from the grave's sky,
and the twenty-four winds

closing all available portals,
the eyelids and the intentions
of ships, so that the pulse
of nature can hardly
be counted.

And there is another world,
past the body thought
by the soul as its own,
her commonest garment:
past its near-bys

and far-offs,
like the seed of language
in this one,
the dark-brown
re-enchantment of his voice.

# FROM STUDIES FOR A RUNNING ANGEL

2 *A Chrisom Child*

All the old descriptions of the porch
remark on its blueness; the added twist
of the blue between the marble
and the meandering gold.

It is impossible to tell
from the brocade and feathers
of the robes, wings and hair of Gabriel,
from the tartan cloth of the angel,

whether he has already spoken.
The cushion plays such a very ambiguous
role, and the fall of his hair
may be compared to a crucifix

that previously disfigured the sky.
The wood, cherry, that within so short
a radius, carried death at its heart.
The young saint is weeping

at that view of the holy life
in his mind, like brown wallpaper,
and it is difficult to imagine
how his body fits together

in its heaviness and delicacy,
the underlying silver
of its conventional desire.
Cold still, his thin elbows,

and most extraordinary fingers,
the parchment of the border,
and the one quart of poppy water
re-shaping his head.


### 4 *A More*

The stairs begin with Jacob's Ladder.
They sit in each other's presence
in a room neither can stand up in;
they both have grey eyes.

The earth is spread out below them,
in small vanished areas of green vegetation,
wood sorrel, the herb alleluia, an earlier meadow
where they once stood fully upright.

She is caught with a breath half-taken,
holding a common rose and a pale book.
The pages of the book curl in space.

Her hands, incapable of gripping,
convincingly fold in a backward turn
against the standard furnishings, the bed.

The angel, from the behaviour of the cloth
in his waistband, seems to have no body
beneath his drapery: no feet appear below.

He carries forward his wing and arm
halfway between rising and sinking,
identified by the dove at his ear

which could be the severely damaged goldfinch
the Christ Child holds to his mouth
in the next stained-glass miracle.

What the simplified eyes experience deepest
in this pilgrimage church
whose beauty is strictly outward

is the candle-burned pearl on her head
like a triple head within solar rays,
her badly rubbed star-halo's
long association of vases,

the unfinished, leave-taking wings.

# HAND RELIQUARY, AVE MARIA LANE

God knows that there is no proof
that part returns to wholeness
simply because miracles happen
at a single church-going.

Her verdant branches labelled
with the names of the five senses,
the garden not ours, she prayed
for her illness to last beyond the grave,

and be the unsealer of that tree.
She might have been dead for a week,
though she went on with her deep
dying, her womb a transparent crystal

turning into a brown relic
even before her death. The blinding
beauty of her hood opening
acted upon me as my own ghost

would do, sounding silk,
as with a lifting gesture
she tore off flesh from her hand,
driving wide her middle finger

into the palm of the other.
Till being a vessel, Christ appeared to her
as a dish filled with carved-up bread
so unnaturally sweet, so lightly crushed,

she could quench the tall language
of his image in her mouth,
which was the breast-wound, always on the point
of being taken, in his female side.

# FALLEN GOD
# OF BONE

The slight disquiet—
feeling the inside edge
of the prison of my body,
imagining that you were about to die . . .

at the end of your life,
turning round towards
meanings immediately lived,
admitting that it is a dream,

was a kind of everyday death
on this deserted earth,
the wave bleating
right up to your absence,

tracing that line of foam,
and drawn to those fringes
in the environs of your soul,
at the surface of your body.

I let myself be led
every second,
misunderstanding your desire
as an entire part of your body,

but I say at once
it leads to no harbour,
the fragmented avenues
of the landscape of sensation.

The self is much too real
and you had consecrated it
to silence, though you
keep silent in very different ways . . .

your gesture of separation
a gesture of overtaking
the very force and treachery
of the separation.

Evening recollection
of the day past,
in a night not soon
to be ended,

the night it denies
lights up the night
from inside, such as
she is, this evening.

You make the truth inside yourself
exactly the same type of light,
and a light seems to tear itself
away from your body and cross the room

where I encounter now my only
language, an eye that opens
at a summit, something prior
to the sentences we speak,

as if, in the eloquent
survival of that voice,
spirit said something
I wanted to say,

whose hand is not light enough,
whose touch is too long,
ever to name that strict absence
our interweaving.

# THE TENTH MUSE

*We must have the arabesque of plot*
*in order to reach the end.* —LORCA


I saw the news of his death
written in white blood
on the grass of Galicia.
It was secret, it was virtuous,
the slight lift of the rib-cage,
the air's last curves
in blood's last rooms
where he performed his dying,
the delicate bridge.

Anything but remaining quietly
in the window, wide-awake,
where daybreak does not enter
and black sounds shake
the low yellow lemons of dawn.
I used to have a sea
where the waves understood each other;
his eyes were two dancing walls
that stirred the plains

and I saw no temple in them.
Deserted blue that has no history.
This sacrament is so difficult—
now they are washing his skin
in oil of white lilies and buttermilk,
eternal skin stopping the mirror
from mirroring.
The water in which his bones
have been washed sleeps for an hour.

And now, with a brief visit
to the cathedral, they bury
his waltzing ribbons in oiled silk,
and the softest pauses
of the veins in his body
that each loved in a different way.
The coolness of reeds swaying
nowhere reaches the dark apple
of his head, his night lying face up,

no blush, ashen-maned,
camellia to be grazed on,
as if a man could outlive
or out-travel his beauty
like gardens. I know very well
that they'll give me a sleeve

or a tie with all its omens
this cavalier winter:
but I'll find him in the offertory,

unbodied arrow in a city of wells,
water-voice the equal
of the Manhattan snow,
unaware that the world is alone
in the sky's other slopes.
What a burning angel turned
to ash I seek, a double
childhood, chameleon
whose branches built a nest!

# POEM RHYMING IN 'J'

The spaces of my blaming soul
were a half-shell of branches, or a rose
of wish, where birds killed themselves
between my eye and its lid.

Touch after touch of pure surfaceness,
the pressure of hand on lap,
the exitlessness from the city much changed
and constantly changing.

I had a way of beginning
like the presence of morning light,
not true morning, in my chanced-upon images,
turned in the hand like votive wax

offering the body whole, to the author of twilights.
I veiled him with my hand from both worlds,
till one third of the night was over,
and the months appeared in human form,

safe passage across that wasted summer,
to fix the destinies for the coming year.
How accidental, your kindest kiss,
the nightingale of your tongue

exactly on a heart like dust, like soil,
with its ruse of affliction as its door.
Words remain on the shore, but when the angel
falls in love, with his different prayer movements,

he is the perfect human.

# The Currach Requires No Harbours

# CONSECRATED WAFER

The side of the world mists,
withholds its broken-necked fruit.
A curtain of freed light
like silk doubled up

(the shape of a woman,
a white leaf painted
after her breast) clouds
the pool's gold-yellow roots.

Water drips from the bark,
the dark mannered woodland bees
falter, as though slowed down by love.
Voices from south of that grove

divide themselves from mouth
to flower to moth,
their lips scoured by Lethe
yet unharmed by the divine.

The venerable skyline
only found by the sea,
that arches from shoulder to shoulder,
seems to shed an eye,

a single, unpaired
violet-lidded eye,
receiver of colour,
and places it outside itself

like ineffectual wings,
the way the moon attaches
her self-closing, liquid glance
to the perfect leaf,

mortal, suffering, in its
throwaway gracefulness,
but sweetened by its marigold colour,
the only colour the dead can see.

# A BOOK OF RAINS

Sheer weather, weather that can be felt
with the eyes, as snow-cover,
selling spring, the first climax
of the year.

Bending, turning, standing,
walking with closed eyes,
the pendent half-moon
pupil in her eye

composes a path
that does not stop unless
forever, patches of her
knowledge blasted away.

Where one would expect
added red, or a hat
of darkness, the line is traced
in the trajectory of the blow

that was dealt. Having nothing
at its disposal
to not yield
to the provocation,

the time of dying
cannot give itself
the other shore,
the future that death gives

is not yet time,
when his forsakenness
draws near, under the force
of the lips of the blow received.

# WOOD-CUNNING

Only your eye, your silver eye,
seems to have no sex, its deep look
of dreamy greeting, the sense
of a small bouquet
in its weaker folds.

Your lips, a glass book,
smell of the glass
and beautiful women rest
their weight in silver and gold
on your acute youth.

The paths of your voice,
plentiful and warm,
make love a second begetting
on a hill near the court, silver-footed
as your preference for unrest.

But the vellum is so buckled
in the apple of your throat,
if your lips were to expire
in a tight, dark strap
tomorrow night,

the echo of having known you,
chieftain-to-be and amateur poet,
would travel together with every
legal and official kissing
like a spear barely missing a plait of hair.

# KADDISH

An angel chances to mention it,
blowing imaginary dust
off the palm of her hand.

Her spine of purple linen,
her eyebrows sewn in a line
in the afternoon, without looking.

Her six small braids shine harshly
in one direction only,
away from my door,

my heart that burns like an oven
where the dead are locked,
till cold or warm memory

lengthens out their shadow
or buys them prayer.
I had come to visit her

wearing an indigo skirt
that she coveted,
her desiring left its mark

on the child like glass in her womb.
Now I do not see any colourableness
in empty winds that could be

spirit-laced, the turning over
of the world by ankle-bells'
sheer fabric-lack.

# HOUSE WITHOUT EYEBROWS

I will remember, with my entire body,
how you were torn. It was wind-still.
A room of idols. You were light blue
on the inside, drowning in darkness;
the sun also spread a despairing
light for me. Great sheaves of lightning
stroked your neckless face, your straight
throat, your small, smooth head,
your yawning eyes, wide-open hands.

They brought a blue-green aura to your upper body
though you were brown-violet on the outside,
with a darkened alertness, without blue,
not an atom of blue, the blue well taken out,
the blue fog of your dress a muffled creeping
in the breathed yellow of your blouse.

But your arm, made up of all whiteness,
underfed, warmed its sleeve,
your hair, unwound, touched the ground
like a track in snow or a coin's embossment.
A dance comes to mind
though the blood-red words of your skin
stand in the worn grass and have no wings.

# THORN PIECE

Cracked flutes close up by lying in water:
her body far, a paste of dust, a stranger
here and there, would need shores of oak
for the slackest share of pear light, moonlight of sound.

With her other face she is gazing,
a woman in communion with herself, her reclining friend,
since sleep, the bringer of light, has no plural,
and fastens her occasional drunken glance
at the touched hand of the snowstorm.

Every imaginable heartache
that could take place in summer
filled the first twenty feet of the spire
with fever of a mild, continuous character,

lifting the knot at the breast of March
where her arms form a basin
torn up by so many years,
off the shape of its hinges.

# MY MUST

An early ray of death
falls on her, my remaining
everlastingness, lime
and red, at her shoulder
the veil changes to deep blue.

It strikes into the evenness
of the day when there is no
weighing, an always
polishing her otherness, in each
occurrence of drawing near and apart.

Till she is more sensitive to time,
of the same blood, a chaos
of smaller willings, alone
with her nowhere,
with this 'with' and 'and'.

Reality is when it happens
a second time, to complete people;
summer is completely male,
my must, he is the I
that makes us into you.

# THE CURRACH REQUIRES NO HARBOURS

Infinite racy stir of water.
The rushes became too dense
in the narrow band of soft earth.

A strange hill rose out of the waves,
the island alive and breathing
with delicacy and a sense of space.

There was no current strong enough
to carry me away. There was no street.
The low-slung horizon, never perhaps before so easy,

sabotaged the once-upon-a-time
in a mood of misgiving or the melancholy
of all fragments. I saw her lover

dressing up as a bird, his bride, his vigour,
her old detached griefs and new overlappings,
before she was betrayed by the bare branches.

# LEMON WITH
# WHITE JUG

The ghost island passes us by,
its Greek name, meaning watchful,
like a cloud bent back upon itself
blown smooth by the wind.

Its village, furrowed with cold,
lays a bed of colour
in the unaccepted space between
your upper eyelid and eyebrow—

doors of lawless scarlet,
a purple that can be tied.
Now a dream begins to value
the fretwork of the small red crowd

to its $n$th foundation, the cool,
bleached mood in the languish
of your neck, the gospel-net
fletching of your arms.

While love (and its technologies)
drinks the working day from your palms.

# REGAINING CONTROL
# OF THE NIGHT

Days that belonged to war and peace
at the same time, they were always so:
darkened cinemas, the strength of lamps
reduced as low as possible.

Peace being restored at different speeds,
the sea disarmed, England calm,
and the shelf upon which it sat
more certain of the greens and golds,

or what she might look like
while looking—her hummingbird nature,
her maple-tree nature. Hers is the first
of many languid arms to reach out

like a lifted horizon in a landscape's
perfect swaying, her opaque red plumage,
lips and heels like patched sails
in the same damp winter's afterglows.

An eye of inshore trees and shrubs,
it has in fact got brighter,
light creeping in directly
in front of the house, a burst of light

over it. Puckering her shoulder,
spreading her fingers,
knifing along the tip
of the beauty leaf on her breasts.

# My Love Has Fared Inland

# PAINTING BY
# MOONLIGHT

It was a bright inviting, freely formed,
though I suppose it was I who brightened,
with an internal scattering of light,
as though weather maps were more real
than the breath of autumn.

The low colourfulness
of the broken and dying leaves
was no embrittlement
to every decided colour on the sunlighted grass
and the warm-hued wood of his door.

But with the dust descending
in the glaring white gap
my backbone pulped and I closed up
like a concertina.

His tongue was hushed as Christ's lips
or once-red grapes permitting
each touch to spread only
when the turn of the violet comes.

# PAINTING A VERB
# HALF GOLDEN

The horizon is in danger,
just off the real land grown on.
Thoughts rub against it and it aches
like a poisonous otherworldly
black star.

The wind blows between it
and the steep face of the wave
that changes the way my fingers
are and the feel of the lines
of my skin.

When blue was nothing
I let you turn my wrist white
and scorch my tongue to living silver
with your young gold:
I let a pretty red hold

me like salt on its side,
and when I was alone
blue's opposite
left a naked grey
at the corner of my eye.

The coats of my eye
like a red-blue couple
recycle your shadow, mortal as words,
blue lying on the rose,
an inverted blue tree:

and next to your mouth,
though the rain does not paint softly,
the deepest pen-shaped groove
would be deliberately too light
for wine-press or pine-cone . . .

# SEALED COMPOSITION

*One learns only from those one loves.* —GOETHE

It is a little like returning to life,
with a new spinal cord that reddens your throat,
your untended name, dreaming and probing,
seeing and testing the consolation
of new gospels.

The cloaked girl, all-too-human sharer
of his flaming tomb,
is flower-reading the transfigured
anti-city, lecturing on mercy, a lady
of the mind, his mind's moated bride.

The seraph's second wing
reverses the needle of happiness
at the wrist, a pilot-angel,
an epiphany in black anxiety,
he snaps his helmet shut on his face.

The slowest of heavens, going up
and down another's stairway,
smothers their angelic ivory boat
in cold and intimate brown tones:
their dry lips find themselves on the reached shore.

# BASHALI

I feel he would give it to me in spirit
as rivers carve out kingdoms,
the boulder field near the watermill,
my father's summer land.

He would give it in my children's
father's name, a crucial terrain
anchored and perturbed,
for thinking in spring about fall

and in summer about the purest time
of winter. If this clothed throat
like a nowhere-to-be-found pool
that shelters under the youngest mountain

could be seen the new breaths
of three hundred dark roses'
third day would tell it all,
holding a door in your arms.

# THE REALM OF
# NOTHING WHATEVER

The difference between things
that are really the same is called
Three in the Morning.

The pigeon's bath and the tiger's regard,
the dawn air and the night air,
bird-stretchings and bear-hangings
and pillowed corpse on corpse.

The broken tile sunk
in the wide house
with the desolate side windows
that zero summer,

the pearl forever irritating the oyster
with inexorable tenderness,

the small earth cannot just file past
the bracing flood-breath of another planet
as if nothing has happened.

You do well to fade away
as if at a border crossing,
fashioning your vanishing
to end without force
in a minimum, rocking note.

# THE CLIFF OF THOUGHT OF RENUNCIATION

Slight colour from the weak, late-night sunlight,
lesser reds, like a barely broken dawn.
The ship is like leaf at the island's ceramic rim,
moths circle the net of the wild courtyard.

As it wishes, spring fragrance may cease,
summer-lidded mountains, clearing autumn skies,
an inkling of winter and golden snow
sprout four seasons, all in one sitting room.

Desire steps in, a poorwill entering the door,
his inch-wide pupils resting repeatedly
on the forest geometry of the tray landscape,
his eyes the eyes of a mountain.

He presents his throat like a cherrystone
carved in a hundred facets, the lyrebird
shape of his ear, the fruits and vegetables
that make up the river diary of his head.

And complete in his breast, within him,
a cloud-dream-lake, a cloud-terrace
ladder of spaces, where we sleep together
in the windswept glimmer of shrine lamps.

# SHOT ANGEL

A gentle pink, close to pain,
was making the sky follow
the innards of the landscape.

The sun's intense amber
slipped a near-human warmth
over the handleless door

so that it seemed to clip
and hinge together
in a fan of blue zigzags

like the rowlock of a gondola.
I could see, starting as though
from a cloud, the child's green aura,

the very essence of his head
deep-sheltered in the open curves
of the blankets, his split and drilled

face. And a field with dark edges
in the fusion of his mouth and ear.
One might question the absence of roads,

the funnelling paths
crisscrossed with narrow tracks,
and the stylized spires

in some lesser stone
at the hushed heart of his map.
No map, however exquisite,

can ever show everything,
the wind cherubs tinted
just the red a woman's lips should be.

# THE SIN EATER

Angel of the Agony, I have found
no name for you yet. I am trying
to fix the sounds, but am I really
alone in this unadorned music?

Their long sleeps threw them into
an elbow chair sweetened with my blood,
like a best-selling funeral sermon
or when those seasons are separated from you.

Kneeling down after three steps,
walking backwards all the way,
I heard a military Mass play,
and worked my trust in God into the floor.

Which step was the real death
on the nicely polished marble,
the wild, old-fashioned, secret death,
the oldest death there is?

I closed my eyes with my own fingers
but further opened my haloed body,
the swerves of fantasy docked
in the isthmus of my neck

till the lavender-flowered garden
was more scented
than if I had been blessed
with a fragrant wife.

# WATCHING THE
# OWLS WITH YOU

Only two people are allowed in the room,
a room designed to imprison,
from the dark inside, in the Arab air,
its door wound and closed.

An almost empty coffin,
as if the earth refused to take
what remained, he died indeed
just like the least important human being,

so gently and so quickly!
If your richness were shared with me,
oh churchyard, this extinct
flightless bird that sleeps

twenty hours a day,
this erect, headless spirit
with its hands and feet bound behind,
mystified in time,

would line the exit
with the continued miracle
of his own play-being, no better,
just as I have burned these threads

and they will not come back:
just like a bringing-back,
just as these names are cold,
the names of the horses

and the names of the angels
place the world as a somewhere
deep in this circle of the sky.
But what she knew

of the nature of the sky
and the crushing of the heart
was the failure of place,
confusing two kinds of space:

where the beginning ends,
and where you see the beginnings
of your self being seen—
a difference that is the symptom

of time, in which
the arborescent book
is lost and lost,
and the city is never completely founded.

It is the same for us, half-dwellers,
reporting to the gods
that a fever might be frightened
or a swelling scared,

during the Paschal moon's increase,
for my vigour, my helmsman, my table,
provider of fuel to my broken rooms,
the one gazed upon in the morning.

# MY LOVE HAS
# FARED INLAND

Of December, the tenth day.
The shape of the hill,
the pent-up river,
the course of the stream,
parcelled out once more.

As he gradually
moved north that winter,
swathes in the grass
on two separate slopes
appeared to show the direction
in which that bloom
was already brushed aside.

The raw, scraped,
bludgeoned land
like a windmill
beneath a nutshell
tackled skies within
a paved parlour
and a groomed park

in what had seemed before
idyllic countryside.

# DESH: THE HOMELAND

They have arranged for me to visit the house
in their own dedicated region, an innocent bystander.
Behind the windows it is only marginally warmer
and certainly darker than outside—a mush
of grey and green remains in my mind.
It is a small space, easy to commit to memory,
and easy to play with in one's imagination.
Mentally, I rearrange the furniture, re-light
the room and heat it up. I sit long enough
to imagine their movements on this confined
stage (trust Shakespeare to have been there before)
and conclude that no amount of re-decoration
will turn it into the comfortable salon they deserved.
It is a lesson in modesty—under these tightly
curled stairs they took their meals crushed
by the news of assassinations, or menaced
from within, and no kindness when kindness was due.

From the house of the living I may as well go
to the house of the dead. Gates surround the churchyard,
but they are wide open, there is no cemetery
to speak of, only the character, the mood
of an incorrect city—shrubs and grass and moss

and muddy lanes amid the tall trees. I find
the grave much where I thought it would be,
in the back part, behind the new church,
to the south and east, a vertical tombstone,
unweathered and unadorned, blue and edgy,
its blank page blanching the skin. But how strong,
how precise, how ample! Making wishes more clear
now, what we cry for, across a lifetime.
Besides announcing whose grave it is, that naked
and proper word, the inscription reads 'Caute',
which is Latin for 'Be Careful', printed just beneath
the drawing of a rose.

The startle reflex in the theatre of my body
closes the locks for fear and anger on the maps
of sorrow . . . I look at the child with his long eyebrows
resting on the wing of a swan, where the flags have taken
wing to a brittle star like Sedna, and am reminded
of Descartes' 'He who hid well lived well'.
As I leave my thoughts turn to the bizarre
significance of this burial site—how fitting it all
is, Bento, Baruch, Benedictus, blessed,
all that gossip from deep within the deepest rhymes
and reasons. And without that once, my ever since
feelings are, the quietly hidden insula
may be the most important of all.

# SOUTH OF MARS

It's over now. Part of the story
has disappeared, into the void
of something that has ended forever:
I know the exact place, behind the house,
a place where waves can be counted,
seven hard cold waves,
like the ones in the sea.

Undreamt of blues and marvellous
greys set up a background,
a flat light and a mask of ocean salt,
for a sea full of inlets, harbours
and ravines, shipwrecks and sudden
green splendours: green, I want you,
green, I am half-full of seawater

though far, far from the sea,
and the smoothest stone
is a freshwater myth.
A cool oval breeze reaches me
from the sea, birds can fly in it,
and every half-minute comes the smell
of the sea, newly cleaned, like a loaf of silver.

The sound of the sea fits inside
an orange in a wicker basket,
or your face when it is still wet.
Its fine sand, of which there is very little,
licks the shell of the sunset without
waiting to go in, as if I had
a gold coin in my hand and didn't

know how to let it go.
I'll do the whole thing in one breath,
and soon this house will be happier
and more logical, without the dark
corridor, without its quiet humble plume
of smoke that was warm blood
mistaken inside a windowpane.

When you're all in the door of your house
with that sense of Saturday and garden gate
you'll know there's no place I'd rather live
to finish out the summer, the last days of August
and the blessed September,
above all, waking up,
and finding *that*.

Send me news how the sea is doing,
wave-like wheat and wheat-like wave.

Remember me when you
are at the beach, in that yacht
with the name of an island—
I would like the water to grow calm
for you and send blue telegrams.

My back to the frozen field
and just one star, I have the joy
of thinking very differently than I did
last summer, the year that the pillow
was embroidered. Who would have said
that eight years later I would look
for the timid city on the map

to see the mountain stripped of mist
and *not* look at the sea,
the church tower rock back and forth
over the pitiable houses? A verbal
and musical ruin. I never understood
the number in your address this past
season, your passport of smiles

like a train without wheels
or wheels without a track.
Surrounded by corpulent trees,
as if the tree had just been invented,

the woman who went to gather kindling
on the beach of day sits down
with all the excitement produced by jewels.

But anything is better than to remain
seated in the window looking
at the same landscape and its surprises.
The sadness that slackens electrical lines
can lengthen the radio waves
of its golden poverty. Perhaps
what we thought would cast a thick shadow

will cast none at all. And thirty Aprils
traced by your fingers will sit down
in the shadowless nudity
of the last lamps, letting the things
themselves decide where their shadows
fall, the cool shadow of that blood,
watching all things take flight.

FROM

# The High
# Caul Cap

# THE NTH OF MARCHEMBER

The way she was standing told me
it wasn't worth going to the trouble
of turning on any more lights.

She guards her blouse, momentarily
holding her heart as if caressing a character
in someone else's family romance.

Within her inner theatre, and seemingly borderless
surround, she quivers across the porcelain
of evening—the bed is certainly more

than it needed to be. When sleep undresses
her mind to even make peace with the city of 'I will',
her blood forewarns her

she is out, out of town, I understand, thumb
on the doorbell, outside, overflying a snowy
border, angel and puppet coming together

in an Old Believer Cemetery whose miracles
take place around boats and water.
For something, read a large half,

a whole self too much—light of my life,
the lanugo of her own splendid body
hobbling my life with its bloody repast.

Those flayed surfaces of her hand are washed
four or five times a day, till the accent
of our parents is fully purged

through our father's cast-off Royal Underwood.
Her undeadness, her petrified unrest
is the ending of time within her,

the alleged redemption's
copy of a grievous gift, flinging her
in and out of the downtown.

# A SUPPLEMENT TO
# THE WITHERING

The evening primrose always is,
and always will be, a memento
of what I will no longer enjoy on earth.

The snowdrop of 1786 is not green,
nor is it white, nor gold, nor purple,
but an union or offspring of all these.

Our not-the-daughter, not-the-wife,
wore a headdress named the kitchen garden
with vegetables attached to her sidecurls,

and her gown was a closely detailed
landscape scene, the bottom of her petticoat
had brown hills covered with all sorts

of weeds, many of their leaves finished
with gold. Every breadth had an old stump
of a tree, that ran up almost to the top,

broken and ragged and worked
with brown chenille. Her robings
and facings were little green banks,

her sleeves loose twining branches:
we must build a statue of a lioness with no
tongue, but a bag of poems, to honour her.

# SANDPAPER LETTERS

The post-war driftwood is stored away
in drawers of silence, bled into the rug,
whatever the wave might suppose.

In order to remain in love,
to see the city reshape itself
in the dangerless September,
the last page is written upside down.

Galaxies dissipate, while the new spring
learns tranquil abiding, recent birth
of leaves and breeding of grass
as if painting your hand with warmth,
at least for the sake of spring.

Her eyes gone hyacinth in colour,
she is now able to see an entire garden
instead of bits and pieces of plants,
but fixes her attention for hours
on the whorls of her fingers,
being wistful about being human.

She is afraid of a small piece of chain
that looks out of place in a room

pulsating off and on—trying to keep
everything the same: yellow ladder
against grey wall, silver atoms
on a platinum surface, green
slippers with flowers on them.

She would speak only when certain
music was played: with small auditory
tune-outs in the partly heard song
she starts to daydream, as if she were tuned
to a vacant television channel.

I sometimes hear her total bewilderment
about other people's unbalanced minds
injected suddenly without warning,

the faint pure tones
of her heartbeat in my ears.

# THE MERCYSEAT

Though Sunday my mother begins it.
Her fingers strike each other like wood,
moth-sound to her ear above
in the skymole light. For a year
she has suffered only ginger.

There are large, tear-shaped areas
in her eye viewed from side-on,
however mousy, fin shapes and a trumpet-
void, as though she were living
without a heart, her merest yearning edge.

And sometimes she revolves in bed
like a roast before a fire.
Her Citherean temple is a nest-scene
on a birdlip mirror, a byway
of tenderness, as when arms seem

flung out from a centre.
I have a sort of cobweb feeling
that we understand how much she wants
to be understood, hearing
the grass grow and the squirrel's heart beat.

# THE HIGH CAUL CAP

The October rains set an all-time record:
all arrivals and departures were in doubt;
the airlines were on strike, it seems, in honour
of the water; in raining mountains, bad, sweet smells.

Calm spiders in the morning rivers,
gusts of birds, melody of bells.
When the heavens duly open
dead leaves explode underfoot.

This cold rain, from a cloud that had
unaccountably overslept, overtakes us
every afternoon like a vague
melancholy from some other autumn.

An immense red blossom, whose name
stops just in time, is the last candidate
for light; she pulls herself along like a broken
cricket, past the lifeless houses.

# MASTER OF THE
# FEMALE HALF-LENGTHS

Mother and daughter, you orbit them both
in their tight widowhood. Her bleak indispositions
whistled up my veins as though they were vacating
houses into which we never moved.

She drank vodka out of a salt cellar
under a melon pavilion, or bean shed,
in a grape garden, till the loosened clang
of round-the-clock daylight

prolonged her endurance of drowning.
Eggwhite bursting seas depearled
the ship not made of flesh, began
to remove its more delicate sails

while broom stars fell apart gently.
I went about my stilling, dressed
the chamber, set up the green velvet bed,
and made an end of my Irish-stitch cushion.

I came to keep my fish days,
sent cordials and conserves, a salt-powder
to put in her beer, since her throat
quakes from time to time

as dark tendrils of her brain snowbud
the growth of that violet sunset.

# DORMITION:
# MADONNA WITH TREES

I suppose today is more or less your birthday:
I pray you, send one word
whether I shall maintain your taper in the chapel.

Our mother, who never seemed to sit down,
takes nothing but broth;
she has crazed eyes, her singing voice out of tune

in any case—how did this one find
her speaking voice? She leaves her next thought
unknown, the unshared thoughts

fall through her upper arms
and through my left arm runs
a flood of striped silk.

The next breathing movement
is a halt in breathing: the throttling sentence
pulls itself together and stops

on the threshold of a rimy minerality.
She does not recover
an ordinary life, tightens like stone

or ebony, cracks, bleeds, decays,
splits into at least four of us,
almost not to move and not to end

but only to dissolve
in an elsewhere that racks her.
I am a slow listener,

should anything be too outstretched
for her hands. I had myself wheeled
into that peaceful room many a time.

She is full of clouds, broken, refashioned,
and infinite, her far side shot through
with blue ovals, moulding thus

a cape towards white,
reminding us there are limits
to how long we can follow her.

In the width of the untrimmed window
the sea lies very quiet with a last
essential light in it

where the house shuts up narrow.
We fear her not to be
of our world at all, her winged breasts

pleated and yellow:
time to ripen up to him.
I turn my microphone then

a little over the yew trees,
the willows old as from the middle ages,
all forming a sort of chalice.

She liked to have a line
around her—the line seems guided
by a sweet jubilation where she is not.

It is she who appears
ready to leave—we mainly lose
a music, or a boat sunk

containing her as music.
All of this, her searching odyssey,
her disintegrating voyage,

must be slipped into silk herbs
by the tips of fingers only.
Now all of the bodies

stand to one edge of the drapery,
without releasing, go beyond her,
so that she may stall and anchor there.

# DARK LIPS,
# JADE PILLOW

This end of day the sea arches
spectral waves and a few lingering
souls recall beach-glare
when the sky would have been stronger.

A three-quarter moon of abstract
grey, like a much-needed lung,
as truly alive as any person,
is weighted to the pre-sunset purples.

I take another subtle sky reading,
contrasted with the daybreak sky
some pages back, when clouds aligned,
the come and gone leaf never quite lost.

# THE BLOOD TROLLEY

My mother I did not know at all:
her cameo appearance in the eighteen
frozen mirrors in her room reminded me
of a gold letter on a quartered rose,
of the same pond. Like a heavy mist
at a temperature just above the dewpoint
when its moisture has not yet coalesced
into drops of rain, her heart has moved on,
closed and unblemished pearl beribboning
the four spokes or rays of the name Jesus.

Beloved document, ash, a residue
on the tongue of the mind, punning red
ink roseshape with deep lines
on her brow's flowing blue, her body
is what has mattered there, registering
in its fluency the steady evaporation
of the person into her stony likeness,
leached away like salts out of a rock.
A bittersweet envoy in black stood
in all this black just waiting to be disrobed.

The name of the mortuary was 'Ultimate Succour'.
Through the tiniest slits I have contrived to make
in the folds of the sari over my eyes
I recognized my mother, selling pickles,
sewing padded armbands, walking through
the Ghetto in a light-coloured coat,
wearing thin shoes with straps, with apples
and pears displayed in a window, waiting
for a coin—she hid her pot in fear when she saw me:
was she fetching milk, was there still milk?

Where was the rickshaw intending to bring
the child with typhoid? Only the better
sort of dead had boxes. The corpse-bearers
wore strange rubber gloves that seemed made
of wood. She was still wearing a blouse,
a beautiful woman of over ninety.
I was led by her through those subterranean
galleries many times, to her haunting world
where already the angels had started
to slam their wings.

Now she seems to be driving
a vehicle with a large skull in front,
or walking a skull on a leash
through marshy riches. I have touched death

with her white bonework, seen dark
things as bright, enchanted by the pleasant
shadow of the rich Christ, saying Peace,
Peace, when there is no peace:
no function for the heart to serve
the dear, the best-known face.

# THE FLOWER OF THE MOMENT OF WHAT COMES EASILY

She sleeps in respect to herself,
languorous and numbed by the pure
when and where. Her sandal
is without power to mark sound.

She cannot avoid this haunting
to destroy her surface self by as many
resurrections as abandonments,
a swan by day and a young woman by night.

Her image on the window glass jangles
into my room, in the most choked
of voices says nothing to me,
a bandage that the flesh has grown over.

Even the daylight feels as mute
as the fourfold halo of the May moon
or the thoughts we say are ours
when stars lose their nests,

pearl-like letters hidden down
a mineshaft. A storm draws up
that swaying blue sky, its thunders
stolen by plumes of explosions

in pear-shapes like poplars. Thus
the unknown rhythm of her looks
is softly spilled in the youth
of the water, metal-skinned.

When someone refuses to meet
one's eyes, in the long now,
across my face stripes the forever
tangible gaze of my late mother.

# SELECT BIBLIOGRAPHY

*The Flower Master.* Oxford: Oxford University Press, 1982; Reprinted as
   *The Flower Master and Other Poems*, County Meath, Ireland: The Gallery
   Press, 1993.

*Venus and the Rain.* OUP, 1984; Gallery, with revisions, 1994.

*On Ballycastle Beach.* OUP, 1988; Winston-Salem, NC: Wake Forest Univer-
   sity Press, 1988; Gallery, with revisions, 1995.

*Marconi's Cottage.* Gallery, 1991; WFUP, 1992.

*Captain Lavender.* Gallery, 1994; WFUP, 1995.

*Selected Poems:* 1978–1994. Gallery, 1997; WFUP, 1997.

*Shelmalier.* Gallery, 1998; WFUP, 1998.

*Drawing Ballerinas.* Gallery, 2001.

*The Soldiers of Year II.* WFUP, 2002.

*The Face of the Earth.* Gallery, 2002.

*Had I a Thousand Lives.* Gallery, 2003.

*The Book of the Angel.* Gallery, 2004; WFUP, 2004.

*The Currach Requires No Harbours.* Gallery, 2006; WFUP, 2007.

*My Love Has Fared Inland.* Gallery, 2008; WFUP, 2010.

*The High Caul Cap.* Gallery, 2012; WFUP, 2013.

# ACKNOWLEDGMENTS

The editors gratefully acknowledge The Gallery Press for permission to use poems in this volume from the following books published in Ireland:

From *The Flower Master and Other Poems* (1993): "Smoke," "The 'Singer,'" "Eavesdropper," "Mr McGregor's Garden," "Slips," "The Hollywood Bed," "The Sofa," "The Seed-Picture," "The Soil-Map," "The Sunbench," "The Flower Master," "The Flitting," and "The Heiress"

From *Venus and the Rain* (1994): "Ode to a Poetess," "The Sitting," "Aviary," "Isba Song," "Harvest," "Venus and the Rain," "The Rising Out," "Hotel," "Dovecote," "Felicia's Café," and "Lime Trees in Winter, Retouched"

From *The Face of the Earth* (2002): "The Brood-bird," "The Face of the Earth," "The Worship of the Plough," "Navicella," "Image of Migratory Cranes," "High Altitude Lavender," "Valentine Not To Be Opened," "Christmas Eve Sky," "Hesterna Rosa," and "She Is in the Past, She Has this Grace"

From *Had I a Thousand Lives* (2003): "Reading in a Library," "The Deadest Deaths Are the Best," "The Pyx Sleeper," "The Sleep Cure," and "Forcing Music to Speak"

As sections of the introduction are based on the editors' previously published work, thanks are due to Bucknell University Press, Cork University Press, and Wissenschaftlicher Verlag Trier.

Finally, the editors would like to express their gratitude to Medbh McGuckian for her kind help and support throughout this project.

# ABOUT THE POET

Medbh McGuckian lives with her family in Belfast, where she was born, raised, and educated. She graduated from Queen's University Belfast and was the first woman to be named writer-in-residence there. She now teaches creative writing at the Seamus Heaney Centre for Poetry.

She is the author of fifteen volumes, and among many awards, she has received the Eric Gregory Award, the Poetry Society's Alice Hunt Bartlett Prize, the Rooney Prize for Irish Literature, the Denis Devlin Award, the American Ireland Fund Literary Award, and the Forward Prize.